CRUST

From sourdough, spelt, and rye bread to ciabatta, bagels, and brioche by Richard Bertinet

CRUST

From sourdough, spelt, and rye bread to ciabatta, bagels, and brioche by Richard Bertinet

with photography by
Jean Cazals

Kyle Books

For Lola Maude
with all my love

Acknowledgements

Once again I owe a huge debt of gratitude to Sheila Keating for her advice, impeccable judgement, and for doing with my thoughts what I can do with flour and water. To Kyle Cathie for supporting my ideas and letting me get on with it. To Jean Cazals for more beautiful pictures, to Jenny Semple for her fabulous design and ideas, to Sophie Allen for keeping the train on the tracks and to all of the team at Kyle Cathie who have a part in getting my scribbles to the book shelf. To Zed Ondrousek for his invaluable assistance with all of the baking and to Janice Teitzel (our Roo) for being a rock when we needed one—you are always welcome back.

To Elodie Stanley for her advice and input on nutrition; to Bloomsbury Store, Cath Kidston and the Bath Antiques Centre for the loan of their beautiful china, napkins, and "knick-knacks".

To our many loyal customers at The Bertinet Kitchen, and especially those who have come to do our bread classes, often from a great distance, all of whom have helped us identify the issues that they and others face when baking at home and to the Barson and Page families for being my taste test panel.

Finally, to Aude Lebesgue for her support at home while we worked on the book and to Jo and the children, Jack, Tom, and Lola Maude, who make it all worthwhile.

Richard

NOTE: All the preparation timings for recipes are approximate and so they will depend on how long it takes you to work your dough. Preparation timings do not include ferment timings as you may have already made your ferment before you start the recipe. Therefore, please read the recipes carefully before you begin. Richard likes to use weight measurements for accuracy, so please use these if you can in order to get the most out of this book.

CONTENTS

INTRODUCTION

When I wrote my first book, *Dough*, my dream was simply to get everyone hooked on making bread. I wanted to keep everything as straightforward as possible, so that people who never believed they could bake would realise what fun and satisfaction there is from making their own bread. And the feedback I have received has been extraordinary. It makes me very happy when people tell me that something they once thought was too complicated and confusing has become second nature. This email from someone who also came to one of my classes just says it all for me—this is why I love teaching people how to make bread:

"....This morning I rose early, baked solo for the first time, and the entire family sat down together for breakfast with warm bread. It was a fantastic sight! Last night I cleared our freezer of 19 loaves of bread from the supermarket. Now I'm the proud mother in our house."

Getting a taste for baking is a great start, but now I want to show you how to apply the straightforward approach of making simple breads to slightly more complex doughs. Sourdough and croissants, especially, are the things everyone wants to learn how to make. So this book is for those of you who are baking happily, but want to take the journey a little further, to explore some breads that require you to take things more slowly, try a few new techniques, or use different flours—from chestnut to buckwheat, or the unusual red Cabernet grape flour I have discovered.

I've called this book *Crust* because, if you'll forgive the pun, it includes the kind of breads that you can really get your teeth into. Also, a fantastic crust is one of the most significant things about great bread—be it a sourdough loaf or a baguette.

"It doesn't matter where you are, what conditions you're working in, there is always a way to work a little magic with flour and water."

An excellent crust forces you to really chew your bread, and when you chew you produce saliva, which contains the enzymes that break down carbohydrates and get your digestion going properly.

By comparison soft, mushy (and, now, sometimes completely "crustless"), highly processed, additive-filled commercial bread needs little chewing and often isn't digested properly, leaving people feeling bloated, and sometimes convinced they have an allergy to wheat—but more on this later, in Chapter 5.

When you have been baking all your life, working with dough becomes second nature. It goes beyond technique. You get to understand and empathise with the way the dough may behave slightly differently, depending on the temperature in the kitchen or whether it is a stormy or humid day, and instinctively you adjust. Remember we are talking about something organic that changes and

"You never stop discovering different techniques or unusual ingredients that bring a whole new dimension to your breadmaking."

develops and reacts. If I find myself baking in an unfamiliar kitchen—for example, when I do demonstrations, where the atmosphere, let alone the oven, will inevitably be different—I find myself adding a little more water, a little less yeast, reducing the rising time.... When you bake every day of your life, it is as if your brain engages with the ingredients, the ambient conditions, and with the dough you are going to make, even before your hand goes into the bag of flour. It doesn't matter

where you are, what conditions you're working in, there is always a way to work a little magic with flour and water.

All of this is incredibly important when you are working in a bakery, because your customers expect bread of a consistent standard, every single day. In my native France, if your bread is beautiful one day, but less so the next, customers will just go to another bakery. In your home, of course, such degrees of perfection are less important than the fact that you are making something good and wholesome for yourself and your family. And if you follow the recipes and techniques in this book, you will bake very good, tasty bread, regardless of the quirks of your kitchen, or the vagaries of the weather. But you will also notice that on some days the dough behaves slightly differently, or your bread turns out to be better than usual.

So, throughout this book, I want to help you to understand a little more about the way dough works, so that you, too, can begin to make those second-nature adjustments, and bake bread of a consistently great quality every day. At my advanced bread classes, I bore people to death by saying that consistency comes with practice. But it is true. The more you bake, the more you will be comfortable with your dough. Try to build baking into your regular routine.

Personally, if I am baking for the family, I always do it late at night or early in the morning. I never enjoy it as much in the afternoon for some reason. Maybe it is a throwback to my apprentice days when I used to have to get up at 2 a.m. My cat used to wait by my bed and then jump in to get warm while I had to go out into the cold air. But the sharpness of the air always woke me up quickly, so I was alert and ready to start baking.

Just because some of the breads in this book are a little bit challenging, it doesn't mean that I am going to bombard you with complicated terminology and techniques, or that you will need anything other than a domestic oven. All the breads in this book are ones I bake at home.

Just as I do in my classes at the cooking school, I will take you through recipes slowly and simply, and then introduce you to some of the variations on a theme that you can experiment with once you have mastered the essential idea of each style of bread. I'll also give you a few ideas about which breads go best with what food and offer recipes for any leftover bread —in France, we believe that there is a different kind of bread for every meal and I grew up with the idea that no bread is ever wasted.

I hope you enjoy exploring some new ideas, and remember that, even when you have been baking for nearly 30 years, you never stop learning or discovering different techniques or unusual flavors and ingredients that could bring a whole new dimension to your breadmaking. That is the joy of the world of baking—it is like an enormous, colorful, exciting jigsaw that human beings all over the world have been building for centuries, but one that will never be quite complete.

1

TOOLS & TECHNIQUES

You will bake your best bread when you are feeling relaxed and comfortable, and the more you bake, the more you will feel at ease. My way of working the dough, as you will see in this chapter, is the key to light, airy bread, and with a little practice it will seem like second nature. Like all bakers, I create my own comfort zone by having my tools ready before I even roll up my sleeves. Just as an artist has his favorite brushes and palettes, all bakers have their own special tools, collected over the years, which are so familiar they feel like an extension of yourself—and I have included some of my favorites.

TOOLS

One of the great things about making bread is that you don't need masses of special gadgets—just your hands, and a few basic bits and pieces. Having said that, I find that as people do more baking they like to treat themselves to some of the "proper" equipment that a baker would use... .

1. Measuring jug—for weighing and pouring liquids.

2. Stainless steel mixing bowl—Mine is big enough to comfortably hold at least 4kg (around 9lb.) of dough. I use it for mixing, resting, and sometimes also for letting the dough rise. Stainless steel is easy to clean, if I drop it on the floor it won't break, and it's light and easy to lift and move around. A china bowl might look beautiful, but it isn't as practical, and a key part of baking is to feel comfortable.

3. Pastry knife—When I am making things like croissants, where I need to cut a clean triangular shape, rather than use the sharp end of my scraper (see **9**), I use a big-bladed blunt chef's knife so I can use it to cut directly onto my wooden work surface without damaging it.

4. Bread knife—When you make your own bread, I think you owe it to yourself to treat it with respect—so invest in a proper, big, sharp, serrated bread knife.

5. Sharp scissors—Sometimes, rather than using a blade, it is also decorative and effective to snip the top of your bread before baking with a pair of scissors, as I do for Chestnut Flour Bread (see page 100).

6. Pastry brush—For croissants, brioche, etc. which are brushed with an egg-wash (just beaten egg and a touch of salt) before baking.

7. Cooling rack—When bread is hot from the oven it is indigestible (more on this in Chapter 5) so always use a wire rack or wicker basket to cool it down before eating.

8. Baking tray—You'll need these for rising and baking, instead of, or as well as a baking stone (see page 21). Upturned or flat trays without a lip can be used for sliding loaves into the oven, if you don't have a peel (see 17).

9. Plastic and metal scrapers—My plastic scrapers are probably my favorite tools, and are extensions of my hands. I use the rounded end to mix the dough and help turn it out from the mixing bowl in one piece without stretching it. I use a metal scraper or the straight edge of my plastic scraper for cutting and dividing the dough, and the rounded end to scoop it up as the less you handle the dough, the less sticky it is to work with.

10. Digital weighing scales—When you are cooking, you can usually afford some leeway in your quantities of ingredients, but baking is more of an exact science, so it is important to weigh everything accurately. Scales are more reliable than trying to read the level in a glass cup so I even weigh my water, as well as any other liquids and eggs. Why do you need to weigh eggs, you might say? I want to encourage you to use the best ingredients, which means cage-free, preferably organic farm eggs—and these will often vary in size. So while a standard large egg (out of its shell) will usually weigh around 55–60g, that doesn't necessarily apply to a box from your local farm.

11. Thermometers—One to check room temperature and an oven one to check that the temperature inside the oven equates to what it says on your control, because to know the heat is crucial to achieving a beautiful crust. Most ovens have a hot spot so move the thermometer around to gauge the best position for baking your bread. If you are baking several loaves at the same time, you may need to swap them around during baking.

12. Lame—The purpose of slashing the tops of your loaves before they go into the oven is to open up the dough, so that you control the point where the gases escape, creating what bakers call a "burst." By doing this, you also create extra crunchy edges to your crust, which look and taste great. You can use a sharp knife, scalpel, or even a Stanley knife but a razor blade fitted into a handle, known as a lame, is the specialist baker's tool,

and it does the job quickly and cleanly, without pulling or snagging.

13. Water spray—Using a clean plant spray to mist the inside of your oven just before and after you put in your loaves helps to add humidity. This slows down the process of the crust forming, allowing the gas inside the dough to expand nicely. If you don't use steam, the crust forms too quickly and thickly, often giving it a grayish tinge, and your loaf may not burst where you want it to. When you combine steam with the heat of a baking stone, you get something close to the atmosphere inside a professional baker's oven (see also page 22, Misting the oven).

14. Tins—small (for around a 400–600g loaf) and large (800g–1kg).

15. Baking cloths—I have a good stack of thick, natural fiber linen cloths for covering dough while it is resting. You can also use baking cloths for lining baking trays, if you don't have a baker's couche (see **20**). Don't use cotton dishcloths, as the dough will stick to them. I simply shake or brush my cloths well after each breadmaking session and let them dry, since they will have soaked up some of the moisture from the dough. I never wash them, because I don't want to introduce the smell of washing powder which will carry over to my dough. The more you bake, the more the cloths become impregnated with natural yeasts and flavors, and become an organic part of the whole breadmaking process.

16. Bread-rising basket—Again, you don't need one of these—you can just use a baking cloth inside your mixing bowl. Wicker bread-rising baskets are lined with the same material used for couches, and they are perfect for holding big loaves like sourdough as they rise. The wicker allows the air to circulate around the dough and lets it breathe, without sticking, inside its lining. Not all bread-rising baskets are made of wicker. They come in various materials, from plastic to wood, and in different shapes. I have some handmade reed baskets, which were traditionally used in Brittany without a lining. I put my dough straight into them to rise, and as it rises and fills the baskets, the reed imprints its pattern, giving the crust an interesting texture and design.

17. Wooden peel—This is what bakers use for transferring risen loaves onto the hot baking stone or tray in the oven (see page 22) and pulling them out again to check they are baked. You could substitute a flat-edged baking tray, or a lipped tray turned upside down, but a wooden peel is perfect for sliding the loaves into the oven easily and quickly, so the oven door is open for the minimal time, and you don't lose heat. Peels come in different shapes and sizes, according to whether you are using them for loaves or baguettes. However, you don't have to buy ready-made ones—you can easily make your own from pieces of plywood (for baguettes, you need pieces roughly 40cm (16in.) long by 10–12cm (4–5in.) wide). What makes the perfect long peel is the lid of a wooden box that holds a magnum of champagne.

18. Rolling pin—I prefer wooden rolling pins, because I like the natural feel of wood. Mine is very special to me because my grandfather made it for me when I was 16. Choose a good solid rolling pin, not too thin, and of a size that feels comfortable in your hands. You will need it for rolling the dough in some recipes, and for making Pain Brie (see page 97).

19. Soft brush—Buy a little natural fiber hand-sized brush, like the one you might use with a dustpan. You can keep it exclusively for baking and use it all the time to brush away excess flour from your work surface. I use nothing but my brush and scraper to keep my work surface clean until I have completely finished my breadmaking for the day. Only then do I wash the surface thoroughly with soap and water, otherwise the smell of soaps and cleaners permeates the dough.

20. Baker's couche—This is a heavy canvas or linen cloth, made from untreated natural fiber, which is used for laying your shaped loaves on while they rise. Because the surface is quite rough the dough won't stick to it. The cloth is stiff enough to be pleated to keep baguettes or rolls separate, or you can use it to line a wicker bread-rising basket (16). A couche isn't essential—you can use a baking tray lined with a baking cloth instead—but this is one piece of equipment that I find people enjoy using. Brush and dry your couche after each baking session.

Timer—A mug of coffee is an essential tool in my kitchen... and yes, I forgot to put a timer in the main picture, which just goes to prove my point that even when you have been baking all your life, you can forget to time your bread. There's nothing worse than spending a morning happily making and rising your dough, only to leave your bread in the oven until it is black because you forgot about it. Seriously, don't assume you will remember to take it out—time it!

INGREDIENTS

There are some fantastic strong bread flours being milled in the British Isles and the U.S., in very careful, traditional ways by millers who know how to treat the grains with respect, retaining much of their natural goodness. These days, such flours aren't difficult to get hold of and most can be ordered online and delivered by post (see page 156 for stockists).

Flour

1. White bread flour (also called strong flour)—For most breads you need good-quality, high-gluten hard-wheat bread flour (organic, if possible, so that the wheat crop hasn't been subjected to chemicals), which is higher in protein than ordinary white flour. This means that during the process of making the dough more gluten is formed, which makes the dough more elastic, helps it to rise better, and results in a light, airy loaf.

The flours I use come from small, artisan mills such as Shipton Mill in Tetbury, Gloucestershire, England (which also imports specialist ciabatta and 00 flour from Italy) and Bacheldre Watermill in Wales. These traditional mills stone-grind the grains slowly in the old-fashioned way, rather than using the big steel rollers favored by large, commercial operations. Stone-grinding keeps the temperature down and the proteins stable. The result is a natural bread flour which doesn't need any of the additives or "improvers" often used by bakeries to help commercial flours perform better. Good-quality, stone-ground flours won't have been bleached or treated with heat to whiten them, so they tend to have a creamy-ivory color and that great smell of wheat.

2. Seeded—In my recipe for Seeded Bread on page 78, I suggest you make up your own combination of seeds to mix into the flour. However, if you want someone to do the work for you, you can buy stone-ground white bread flour that also contains seeds. To use a seeded flour in the multi-seeded bread recipe, just add up the quantity of flour and seeds in the list of ingredients and substitute the same amount of seeded flour instead.

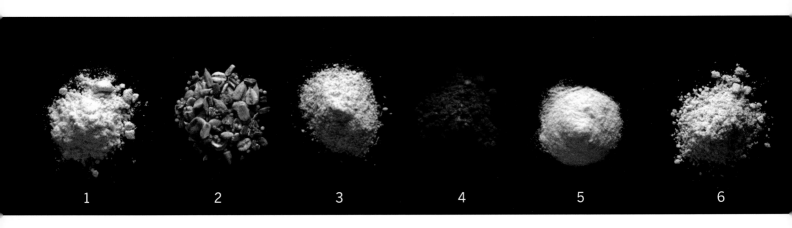

1   2   3   4   5   6

3. Rye—This always adds flavor and character to your bread. I like to use dark rye but usually combine it with white bread flour—as little as 30–40g (1–1$\frac{1}{2}$ oz. or $\frac{1}{4}$–$\frac{1}{3}$ cup) of rye will make a difference to the taste of your bread—as 100% rye can be quite heavy, unless you use a ferment (see page 47) to help lighten it.

4. Red Cabernet grape—This really unusual flour from Canada isn't made from grain at all, but from the dried and powdered skins of grapes left over from winemaking. It has a fantastic rich red color that carries over into the bread, giving it a real depth of "winey" flavor (see page 89 for recipe).

5. Fine Semolina—I like to use fine semolina to dust my peel (see page 14) before I put the risen loaves onto it ready to load them into the oven. The grains are like little pearls which help the loaves to slide easily from one to the other. You can use ordinary flour but, since it burns more quickly than semolina, it can give a darker look to the bottom of your loaves.

6. Wholemeal—sometimes called whole-wheat, this flour is often seen as the most healthy as it contains the whole grain, whereas a brown flour contains around 85%, and white flour 75–80%.

7. Spelt—I love the flavor of spelt. It is an ancient grain of the wheat family that is even mentioned in the Bible. For a while it was out of favor, as the world opted instead for modern, more prolific and easier to grow species of cereal grains, but now its slightly nutty flavor is very much back in fashion. Although spelt flour contains gluten, it is less strong and more fragile than is usual in flour, so people with wheat, rather than gluten, intolerance might find it more digestible.

8. Khorason (or Kamut)—This is another ancient wheat which, like spelt, fell out of favor and has been reborn. In the U.S., where it is grown organically in Montana, it is called Kamut, and the story is that it was used in ancient Egypt and rediscovered by an American airman in the 1950s. However, where I buy the flour, they have done their research and discovered that its true name is Khorason, and it probably originates in northern Iran. In parts of the Middle East and Central Asia, it has been grown in subsistence farming systems for centuries. The flour is slightly more fibrous than wheat flour, with a sandy golden color and a lovely earthy flavor—almost a taste of the fields. You can use Khorason on its own, but it contains a less strong form of gluten than wheat, which can make for heavy bread, so I find you get much lighter results when you blend it with white bread flour.

9. Cornmeal—This is milled from corn (sometimes called maize meal) and is used for polenta. I use it instead of flour to dust my ciabatta before baking as it gives a beautiful finish to the loaves.

10. Chestnut—This comes from France or Italy mostly, is often only available seasonally and may be in short supply, so can be quite expensive, but it gives a fantastic flavor to your bread and is also gluten free.

11. Oats—I like to add oats to my mix of edible seeds when I make Seeded Bread (see page 78). You can also roll the top of rustic looking breads in oats before baking.

12. Buckwheat—Most people think of buckwheat as an American crop used for pancakes, but it is also traditional in Brittany where we use it to make savory galettes. In France, it is known as sarrasin after the Saracens, Arab invaders who may have introduced it to Europe in the 15th century. Despite its name, buckwheat isn't wheat at all, but the fruit of a bushy plant related to rhubarb and sorrel. Because it doesn't contain gluten, it doesn't rise —unless you combine it with white wheat flour—which is why it is typically used in flatbreads and crêpes that are cooked on a griddle (originally, probably, just on a hot stone). I use buckwheat with white and rye flour in my Breton bread (page 86), and for Blinis (page 109). It adds a subtle, slightly sour flavor. which works especially well with seafood.

Other ingredients

Yeast—Yeast is amazing stuff. It belongs to the fungus family and apparently ten billion cells are needed to make a single cell of fresh yeast. The recipes in my first book, *Dough*, used fresh yeast, which is made from cells cultured in a laboratory, but in this book I will also be introducing you to natural yeasts, which like those used in making cheese or beer, will breed and multiply if you give them the right conditions.

Personally, I rarely use dried yeast because I find it tends to be too strong in terms of flavor and activation. However, there is no harm in having some in the cupboard just in case you need it. If you do use dried yeast, buy the "easy-blend" type and halve the ratio of yeast to flour recommended on the pack. Instead of dissolving it in warm water first, just rub it straight into your flour as if you were making a crumble. You don't need to add any sugar because there is enough natural sugar in the flour to feed the yeast. By using less yeast and not over-feeding it with extra sugar, you will help the yeast to react more slowly and stop it from becoming too powerful.

A simple and basic rule, whether you are using fresh commercial yeast or dried yeast, is that the less you use, the longer the dough will take to rise, but the flavor will be better developed and the bread will last longer. Conversely, the more yeast you use, the quicker the dough will rise, and as a result your loaf may be brick-like and yeasty tasting, and will go stale much more quickly.

Water—Some bakers insist on using bottled water, but personally I have no problem with tap water, unless you live in an area where the chemicals used to clean it give it a harsh taste—in which case filtering it first should help.

The water, unless a recipe says otherwise, should be at body temperature, which means that if you put your fingers into it they won't feel either hot or cold. That said, in extreme temperatures, you may sometimes need to use cooler or warmer water (see page 41). I weigh my water so it is measured in grams rather than milliliters.

Salt—Much has been written about salt and its overuse in recent years. It is easy to demonize it and forget that without it we would, quite literally, die. In breadmaking, salt is important because it helps to stabilize the fermentation, improve the color and flavor, develop the crust, and conserve the bread. Without salt, bread will become stale and dry much more quickly. Sometimes in my bread classes people say: "20g of salt (4 teaspoons) in 1kg of flour ($7^1/_3$–$7^2/_3$ cups)? That's a lot!" But you have to remember that that amount of flour will give you 2 large loaves, or their equivalent, so the quantity of salt in each slice of bread is relatively little (see page 48). Of course, you can reduce the levels of salt in the recipes if you want to, but you may find that the dough rises more quickly and the flavor and color of your finished bread is different.

I feel it makes sense to use fine, pure, natural sea salt judiciously in your breadmaking and when you are cooking with natural raw ingredients, and to avoid the kind of processed foods which are full of salt—and most probably processed salt, stripped of much of its natural mineral content—especially those that you might not expect to contain high levels, such as cookies and cereals (see Chapter 5, for more on this). I usually use sea salt for making dough, rather than coarse salt, which is harder to dissolve. However, one of my favorite sea salts is the large-grained, rustic sel gris, full of minerals, from Brittany, which you will need to dissolve using a little of the water from your recipe before adding it.

Eggs—Good eggs make all the difference. Compare the deep golden color of the yolks of eggs from hens that have been allowed to run around and forage freely, to the anemic pale yellow yolks of hens from overcrowded battery cages, and you will be amazed. It isn't just the color, but the flavor, and the strength of the albumen, that is so much more powerful when eggs come from thriving hens, especially the old-fashioned breeds which aren't cross-bred to lay eggs constantly. I buy from local farms, as well as from Clarence Court, in England's Cotswolds, who produce beautiful blue and green eggs from Old Cotswold Legbar hens and dark brown ones from Burford Browns, and Columbian Blacktail eggs. The depth of flavor, color, and sheen they give to a bread like brioche make the small extra expense well worth it, not to mention the welfare of the hens. As I said on page 12, when you buy good farm eggs they tend to be different sizes, so in all the recipes in this book that use whole eggs I have given a shelled weight, as well as an approximate quantity, since weighing your eggs is far more accurate.

Butter—Most of the recipes use unsalted butter, though the Pain Brie on page 98 calls for a good Breton, salted butter, the kind I was brought up on—and which I still think is fantastic. The best breakfast, for me, is a lightly toasted slice of sourdough with salted Breton butter. And I love it on scones, too.

Salted butter is softer than unsalted, so it doesn't work for croissants, where you need your butter to be as hard and cold as possible. For croissants, especially, where you really taste the butter, the quality is crucial. A lot of

croissants in British supermarkets these days are made with something called "concentrated butter" (you'll see it listed on the labels), which has carotene in it to make it a bright yellowy-orange color that is supposed to make the croissants look more attractive. Personally, I think it just makes them glow unnaturally, as though they have been lying on a sunbed!

My favorite butter for croissants and pastry is unsalted, fresh and creamy French Appellation d'Origine Contrôlée from Normandy or the Charente. In the Charente, they say that it takes 1,000 liters of milk to make 100 liters of cream to make 10kg of butter (which converts to 264 gallons of milk to make 26¼ gallons of cream to make 22 pounds of butter). The best butters from both regions have a wonderful creamy taste when raw, which becomes nutty and refined when you bake with them. That's not to say there aren't plenty of lovely and often very different styles of other butters out there—it's just that I tend to stay with French butter for croissants. If I am making scones or Bath Buns (see page 140), I usually use English butter. Taste as many good butters as you can, find the ones you like, and stick with them.

WORKING WITH YOUR OVEN

Often people don't believe that you can bake good bread in a domestic oven. When I teach my bread classes we use typical ovens, the kind that everyone can relate to, nothing cheffy or "baker-ish." However, you need to maximize the potential of your oven by preheating it really well, using a baking stone, spraying the oven with water when you put in your bread, and most importantly making sure you don't waste heat by leaving the door open for any longer than necessary.

Preheating—Dough is at its most responsive in a warm atmosphere so you need to heat up not just your oven, but your whole kitchen as early as you can. Usually when I bake, the first thing I do when I get up in the morning is to put the oven onto its highest setting (250°C/500°F, if possible). For some of the recipes, you will need to turn the oven down to a lower temperature just before you put the bread into the oven; for others you can leave it at this heat. If you are going to bake your bread directly on a baking stone or tray, put this in as soon as you switch on the oven so that it too gets really, really hot.

Using an Aga—When I moved from London to a house in Bath, I found myself with an Aga for the first time. While I did manage to make very good bread, especially small loaves, even though the Aga was probably 40–50 years old, we didn't stay there long enough for me to become an expert. So if you want to know everything there is to know about baking in an Aga, I suggest you have a look at one of the many good books on Agas that are around.

All I would say is make sure your Aga is fully hot before you make your bread and try to bake first thing in the

morning (when the oven is at its hottest), rather than at the end of the day when you might have been cooking dinner and the oven might have cooled down. It's a good thing to use an oven thermometer to check the temperature. I also found it advisable not to use the hot plates on the top of the Aga for cooking at the same time, as it drew away too much heat.

My best loaves were made directly on the floor of the top right, hot oven—even better with a hot baking stone inside first. Sometimes the bread would start to brown after 5 minutes, in which case I would prop the door slightly ajar.

Using a baking stone—The idea of using a baking stone is to try to recreate the baker's oven, in which the dough is slid straight onto a hot brick floor, so it starts to bake immediately underneath. Because I tend to bake quite a lot of bread at one time, I use two pieces of granite which live permanently in my oven on two different shelves, so I never have to remember to put them in. The moment I turn the oven on, the stones start to heat through, then when I am ready to bake I just slide the dough onto them using my peel (see page 14). A baking stone isn't essential—you can substitute a heavy baking tray, turned upside down so that it is completely flat, or have one baking stone and use an additional tray when you need it. However, a baking stone will retain the heat better and it is one of those things that I find gives people real confidence in their baking.

Misting the oven—To make bread with a good crust and color, you need to add some steam into the oven as the loaves bake. Just as using a baking stone is the closest you can get at home to the brick floor of a baker's oven, misting creates a similar effect to the steam injection system that professional bakers use to put humidity into the oven.

Without steam, the crust of your loaf will form very quickly, and the expanding gas inside will have nowhere to go. The result is that the crust will burst open—but not necessarily where you would like it to. You will find, too, that it takes on a grayish, rather than a golden, tinge. With steam, the top of the loaf stays moist, delaying the formation of the crust, allowing the gas to expand until the crust bursts, as you intended, through the slashes you have made in the top of the loaf.

Some people suggest putting ice cubes in the bottom of the oven, but I find that this doesn't create steam instantly enough. By the time the cubes have melted, the crust is already starting to form. Others put a lipped tray of water in the bottom of the oven, which can work well, especially if you have a gas oven where the source of the heat is at the bottom.

Misting the oven with a clean plant spray filled with water is by far my favorite way—it's so easy. The more I bake using a domestic cooker the more I am aware that the more you mist the better—it makes such a difference, especially for baguettes. Obviously don't spray so much that your oven is filled with water, but around 15 good squirts before your bread goes in and another 5 after should do it. Get close to your oven when you spray—just a few centimetres away (an inch or two)—you should be able to feel the steam on your hands. And do it quickly, so that you don't keep the door of the oven open for too long.

Loading the oven—It might sound obvious to say: "don't leave the oven door open for any longer than you have to, otherwise you will lose heat," but when I am teaching I find this is one of the hardest messages to get across. Loading your oven should take no more than 15–20 seconds—any longer and you could lose 40–60°C/70–110°F, which robs you of the instant surge of heat that seals the bottom of the bread and helps to form a beautiful crust. The key is to be organized and have a mental checklist: are your loaves on your peel/baking tray? Have you slashed the tops? Are they close to the oven? Is your water spray handy? If the answer is yes to all of these, *then* open the oven door. Mist the oven quickly—15 or so squirts—slide in your bread, give another 5 squirts, then close the oven door and don't do as most people do when they come to classes for the first time—that is, open the oven door again. You will need to check progress towards the end of baking time, but other than that don't be tempted to keep peeking.

WORKING THE DOUGH

I prefer to talk about "working" the dough, rather than "kneading" it, because my technique is very different to the traditional English way.

First you need to mix your ingredients (according to your recipe) in your mixing bowl for about 3–5 minutes, making sure that all the dry bits are incorporated, and everything is bonding. Then, with the help of your scraper, turn out your dough onto your (unfloured) work surface, ready to work it. Get into the habit of scraping out the bowl really well, making sure you don't leave any scraps of dough in there, because you are going to put your dough back into the bowl after you have worked it, to rest and expand to around double its size, so any bits in the bowl that have dried out will attach themselves to the dough and snag its silkiness. (Never wash the bowl until after you have finished baking, as you don't want to introduce any smells or tastes of soaps or sprays.)

Now you need to transform what feels like a sticky mixture into a silky, smooth, lively dough. In England people talk about "kneading," which involves pushing and pummeling the dough with the knuckles and the heel of your hand. My way is very different, and is based on an old French technique from the times when bakers typically had to work around 80kg by hand. It involves stretching and slapping the dough down in quite a dramatic way, so that as much air as possible is introduced and trapped inside, and the gluten stretches, forming a light, lively dough.

It is this technique, which I have adapted to home-baking that allows you to work with wetter, softer dough than most people in England are used to. When I first started baking in England, I was struck by the fact that most recipes required a much lower ratio of water to flour than I had ever used. Often they would also say to add more flour, if necessary. Then you would be told to flour your work surface well to prevent the dough from sticking during kneading. This adds up to a lot of extra flour—and too much flour, to my way of thinking, means dough that is quite stiff and unresponsive and heavy, brick-like bread.

When I work the dough, I don't flour the work surface at all. When people who have been making bread for many years see how much water I use, then start to handle the sticky dough, they often struggle at first as it takes a bit of getting used to, but once they get the hang of the technique and feel the airiness and life in the dough, they never look back.

So, don't flour your work surface—yes, the dough will stick at first, but resist the temptation to dip your hand into the flour bag, because it will come together. You just have to believe!

The technique

Slide your fingers under the dough (opposite page right), then with your thumbs parallel to your index finger-tips (1), lift it lightly (2), swing it upwards (3) and then slap it back down, away from you, onto your work surface (4). Stretch the front of the dough towards you, then flip it back over itself like a wave (5), stretching the dough forwards and sideways and tucking it in around the edges (6).

Keep repeating this sequence (initially, after every 10–15 flips, using your plastic scraper to help you lift the dough from the work surface). The more you practise, the more you get into a rhythm and can

do everything in one smooth movement. The secret is to relax. Don't worry about the stickiness, keep your touch very light and work the dough quickly. Often in classes I see people struggling because they are gripping the dough too tightly, pressing their fingers into it so it gets even stickier. When I step in and work the dough quickly and lightly for a minute or so, they can see the difference immediately as it swells and comes to life.

As you continue to work the dough, it will expand as the air bubbles get trapped inside, and feel silky, smooth, and firm, yet at the same time lively and a little wobbly, and it should come away from your work surface cleanly. If, after you have been working it for 10–15 minutes, the dough is still a bit sticky, don't panic. You've still done enough to get plenty of air through it. Just finish by forming into a ball (see opposite) and next time try to handle it a little more lightly and stretch it a bit more as you work it.

Using a mixer

I prefer to mix and work my dough by hand, but I know that for some people it is easier to use a machine. All the doughs can be done in a mixer with a dough hook and for some recipes, such as brioche, it makes sense, because it is a long process that can seem quite daunting.

I would say, though, that when you first start baking, it is good to work the dough with your hands a few times before switching to a machine, just so that you get the feel of the way the dough comes together and you know the results you are looking for.

I still haven't found a dough hook that can properly handle my kind of very soft dough without having to stop it every so often and scrape the bottom to incorporate the ingredients properly. Also, because I don't feel you can get as much air into the dough as you would by hand, I suggest that even when you do use a machine, once you have turned out your dough onto your work surface, you work it for a minute or so by hand (see page 25) to get a bit more life and air through it.

To mix in a machine, put the ingredients into the bowl and start off at just under number 1 speed. Mix for 4–5 minutes, stopping every so often to scrape up all the dry bits at the bottom of the bowl, so they can be worked in. Increase the speed to $2^{1}/2$–3 for another 7–8 minutes, until the dough comes together.

Tip it out onto your work surface, without any flour, and work the dough for another minute—5 or 6 flips should be enough—then form it into a ball (see page opposite).

A fine dusting of flour...

Once you have worked your dough, *now* you can very lightly flour your work surface. The flour won't affect the texture of the dough, but you still don't want to spoil its smooth surface, so only use a fine dusting. By that I mean that you should hardly see any flour on your work surface, if you were to run your scraper across it, you would gather up a small mound.

Forming the dough into a ball

Having lightly dusted your work surface with flour (1), place your dough, smooth-side down (2), and fold each edge in turn into the center of the dough, pressing down well with your fingers (3) and rotating the ball as you go (4–5). Finally turn the whole ball over and stretch and tuck the edges underneath (6).

RESTING & FOLDING

Once you have worked your dough and formed it into a ball you will need to let it rest in a warm, draft-free place and then, depending on the recipe, fold it, and reform it.

Lightly flour your well-scraped bowl, put in the ball of dough smooth-side up, cover with a baking cloth and let it rest, usually for about an hour (though the time will vary from recipe to recipe), in a warm, draft-free place, during which time it will rise to around double its volume and develop its structure while the flavor matures.

By a "warm place" I mean around 25–30ºC/77–86ºF, which is the temperature in my kitchen after I have had the oven on since early morning. I simply leave the dough on the top of my stove, which is away from any drafts. Other places you could use include a microwave (turned off, of course) or a kitchen cupboard.

Just as the dough needs to be warm so that the yeast will activate and raise the dough properly, it is equally important for it not to be in a draft, as this, too, can cause a skin to form. When you are working in a professional bakery, a draft coming through is the worst thing that can happen, since it upsets the balance and constancy of warmth that is crucial to turning out loaves of a consistently high quality.

Some of the recipes in this book, such as sourdough,

call for the dough to be rested twice or three times throughout the process. In general, the longer the dough is allowed to rest, the more developed the flavor will be, and the longer the bread will last.

Folding—When a recipe calls for the dough to be rested more than once, you need to re-shape the dough in between each resting to reinforce it and help the flavor to develop. This is the point where an American recipe would call for the dough to be "punched down," which roughly translates as punching the living daylights out of it. I prefer to use the term "folding," because what I do is much gentler. I just lightly flour the work surface, then turn the dough out of the bowl, with the help of my scraper, so that the smooth, rounded side that was uppermost in the bowl is now underneath. I flatten it down a little with my fingertips, then fold the outside edges in on themselves a few times, pressing down gently each time, and rotating the dough as if forming a ball (see photograph opposite and page 27). Then the dough can go back into the bowl (again lightly floured) to rest again, according to the recipe.

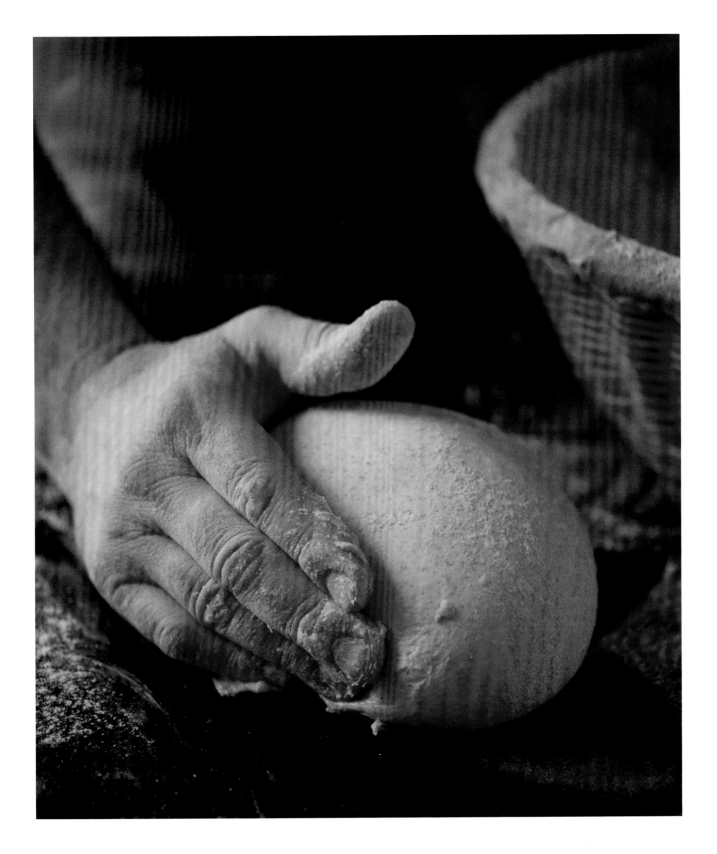

DIVIDING THE DOUGH

Your rested dough will now be full of life and responsive, ready for you to turn out and divide up to make loaves, baguettes, or small rolls.

Whenever you need to divide a large piece of dough into any more than two pieces, very lightly dust your work surface with flour first. When I'm teaching I find that, after managing not to use too much flour on the work surface up to this point, once people start cutting the dough, and feel it getting a bit sticky again, they tend to relapse and start putting their hands in the bag of flour. So really try to persuade yourself not to, so that you preserve the smoothness and sheen of your dough.

With the help of your scraper, turn the dough out of the bowl, smooth-side down, onto your work surface (1). Press gently into a rectangular shape. With the long side facing you, fold one third into the middle (2) and press down with your fingertips. Then fold the other side into the middle and again press down (3–4). Next bring the top edge of the dough over the top and tuck underneath to seal (5). Turn the length of dough over, so the seam is underneath (6). Now you are ready to divide it.

Have your scales ready. In my first book, I generally left it to you to decide whether to weigh the pieces as you divided the dough into pieces for rolls, or baguettes. However, as you bake more, you'll find it pays to be a bit more precise and keep your loaves or rolls all the same size, so that when they are in the oven they will all bake at the same rate. Otherwise, you will lose heat opening the oven to take out smaller loaves or rolls which will be ready first.

So, in this book, I want to encourage you to use your scales. Use the sharp end of the scraper to cut each piece of dough (7), and then lift it up with the scraper. As you are using the minimal amount of flour on your surface, this will help you to lift the pieces cleanly without them clinging, keeping the springiness in the dough. If a piece sticks and you start clawing at it with your hands, you will only make it even stickier.

It might sound pedantic, but it's good to get into the habit of keeping each piece of dough upright—that is, with the smooth side upwards—when you put it on the scales, and when you lift it off ready for shaping. That way you handle it as little as possible.

Cut one piece at a time and then weigh it (8–9)—don't cut all the pieces at once—because unless you have an incredibly good eye you won't be that accurate in your cutting when you start out, and you will end up with lots of scraps of dough as you try to make adjustments. Once you have been baking for a while, though, you will find that you can gauge weights fairly instinctively. I challenge myself to try and get it exactly right every time! So, cut and then weigh, cut and then weigh…. If a piece of dough is underweight or overweight, either cut a little off with your scraper, or cut a bit from the main piece of dough and add it on. As you go along, make use of the scraps so that as little dough as possible is wasted. Now you are ready to shape your dough.

SHAPING THE DOUGH

In a bakery we would use the term "molding" for the process of forming loaves or rolls—however, I find that people relate much better to the simpler idea of "shaping."

Before you start shaping your dough into rolls or loaves, have your baskets or pans ready to hold them while they are rising (see page 36). Good baking is all about being organized and thinking one step ahead.

If you are making large loaves, prepare your bread-rising basket, couche, or bowl lined with a baking cloth with a light dusting of flour (unless the recipe calls for a long rising time, in which case you will need to dust more heavily). If you are baking in pans, make sure they are lightly greased with vegetable oil or butter.

If you are making rolls or baguettes, line a baking tray with a couche or baking cloth and again lightly dust it with flour. Once you have put in your first row of rolls or baguettes, you can make a pleat in the cloth before putting in the next row to keep them from touching each other as they rise.

Also have some extra baking cloths ready to put over the top of your dough as it rises.

Shaping into loaves

When you start to shape your dough into a loaf it is important to get some strength into what I call its "spine," so that the bread holds itself firm.

To do this, first lightly dust your work surface with flour. Take your piece of dough and place it, smoothest-side down, on your work surface and flatten it with your fingertips into a rough oval shape.

Fold one side of the flattened dough into the middle (1) and press down quite firmly with the tips of your fingers. Bring the other side over to the middle and again press down firmly (2–3). Now fold the bottom edge into the middle and press down (4), then repeat with the top edge (5). You should be able to see clearly the indents of your fingertips forming the "spine." Fold over in half and then press down again firmly to seal the edges (7–8).

Finally, turn the loaf over so that the seam is underneath and either place it in a greased loaf pan (9), on a couche, or in a lightly floured wicker bread-rising basket, or bowl lined with a baking cloth.

Shaping into rolls

Using the same technique as on page 27 (Forming the dough into a ball), fold each edge of the dough one at a time into the center and press down well with your fingers, rotating the ball as you do so. Turn the ball over and, cupping your hand over the top, roll it with your fingers until it is round and smooth (you can see me doing this on page 135 pic 4). When all your rolls are shaped, lay them on a baking tray lined with a lightly floured couche or baking cloth.

Shaping into baguettes

Since the characteristic of a baguette is that it is long and thin, it is extra-important to get some good strength into its "spine."

As for shaping any loaf, dust your work surface lightly with flour, flatten your piece of dough with your fingertips (1), then fold one side into the middle and press down firmly (2). Fold the other side into the middle and again press down firmly (3).

Finally, fold the dough in half lengthways towards you to form a long log shape. If you are right handed, starting at the right end of the dough, hold the edge of the dough between the forefinger and thumb of your left hand (4) and twist the dough slightly towards you, then press down with your right thumb (5–6). Work this way all along the length of the dough. This slight twisting movement will give the edge more strength than if you just crimp it with your fingers to seal it as you would for a more chunky loaf (7). Work as quickly as you can—the less time you spend handling the dough, the springier and more responsive it will be and the less it will stick to your hands.

Turn the baguette over so that the seam is underneath, and then roll the top very lightly and quickly with your fingertips. Don't press down or you will flatten the life out of it—you just want enough light touches to loosen the dough. Place on your lightly floured couche or cloth-lined baking tray (8–9).

If you are making more than one baguette, make a pleat in your flour-dusted couche or baking cloth to keep each one separate.

Cover with another baking cloth and let rise according to your recipe.

SECOND RISING

This is the time when the dough is left to rise again, after it has been molded or shaped into loaves or rolls. Once more, it will rise to just under double its volume.

The breads in this book usually take between 1 and 2 hours to rise a second time (in the same place you rested your dough earlier), depending on the recipe and the temperature in your kitchen. The reason I say "just under" double its volume is that until you get a feel for baking, it isn't always easy to gauge that moment when the volume of your dough has doubled. You will get better results if you slightly under-rise your dough (it will still rise and burst open on the top) than if you over-rise it, in which case it is more likely to collapse—leaving you with something that resembles a brick.

Retarded second rising—This is simply a method of letting your dough rise overnight in the fridge, rather than at room temperature. The longer fermentation gives a really good flavor and crust, though it's not practical all the time as you won't always want to wait 24 hours before you bake. You might like to try it if you have more dough than you want to use in one day.

Put the dough on a lightly floured couche or in a bowl lined with a baking cloth and cover it with another baking cloth, as before. Put in the fridge for 12 hours or overnight, allowing an extra hour for it to return to room temperature before you bake it.

ACHIEVING THE CRUST

A great, tasty, crunchy crust is the product of various things: a well-worked, smooth airy dough that has risen well without drying out or forming a skin on top, a good misting in the oven, some serious heat, and the careful slashing of the top of your loaf.

Savoring good food begins long before you put it in your mouth. It is to do with aroma, and the way it looks. A rustic loaf with a wonderful crust invites you to eat it. And a big part of achieving a great crust is slashing the top of the loaf so that the gas that expands upwards as it bakes will have some-where to escape and break through, in what we call a "burst." The way you slash the top of your dough controls where that burst will happen as well as how the finished loaf will look.

Sourdough loaves are probably the most famous for their appearance— very often the designs that are cut into the tops of the loaves look all the more dramatic because of the traditional dusting of white flour against the dark color of the bread.

In France the story behind the marking of sourdough is actually a practical one, dating back to the days when very few families had ovens. Instead, they would make their bread and take it down to the local baker who would bake it for them. In order to be able to recognze their bread when it came out of the oven, each family would carve their initials, a crest, or some identifying mark into the top of their loaves. Overleaf you can see some before and after pictures of classic sourdough decoration. Or you can create your own signature.

Traditionally bakers use a lame (see page 13) for slashing the tops of loaves, but you can use a sharp knife or a pair of scissors. The important thing is to make your cuts quickly and cleanly, with the tip of the blade, so as not to pull and drag the dough.

To slash baguettes, use your blade to make diagonal cuts along the top. In France, a baguette from a bakery must weigh 320g (11 1/2 ounces) and have 7 cuts. Make your baguette as long or short as you want, and make 5 or 6 slashes if you prefer—less, maybe, for small ones.

WHAT ABOUT THE WEATHER?

When you bake regularly, you will probably find that at some times your dough is more responsive than others. Often this is related to whether the atmosphere is cold or hot, humid, or dry. With a few adjustments, however, you can have consistently good bread every day.

Bakers always talk about the weather, the way it can affect dough, and what compensation they can make. It is one of the things that people read a little about, and then feel very confused, so in my first book, *Dough*, I made no reference to the weather at all because all the doughs I make and the techniques I use are forgiving enough to give you good bread irrespective of the conditions in your kitchen. By just following the recipes in this book you will make very good bread, but you also have to remember that everyone's kitchen will be slightly different, just like their ovens.

Furthermore, as you bake more often, you will begin to notice that on a hot day, for example, the dough might develop more quickly than you expected, or if it is stormy outside it might seem unusually "sweaty" and sticky and harder to handle. Maybe on some days you are more pleased with the results than on others. So part of being comfortable

with baking is getting used to making small adjustments—most of them just common sense—in order to get consistently good results every time you bake. In Brittany they always used to say that in the old days when the weather got cold, in order for the bread to rise, people used to put the big reed baskets full of dough under the marital quilt! I'm not suggesting you go that far, but you will find that with practice and experience, you will be able to troubleshoot, as if it were second nature.

I often suggest people keep a little diary when they start baking, noting down the weather, how the bread came out, and how the dough behaved. If necessary, you can then use the adjustments opposite to compensate for any weather-related problems. The symbols refer to your kitchen at ambient temperature (i.e., with no air conditioning and without the oven being put on to warm up the room).

WEATHER CONDITIONS	ADJUSTMENT
Hot, bright sun If your kitchen becomes hot and dry in these circumstances, unless you have enough water in your dough, the resulting bread will be heavier, tighter, more yeasty, and not as well developed as usual. Essentially, you need to slow things down.	• Use cold water • Add an extra 20–30g (about 1½–2 tablespoons) water to make the dough a bit softer • Reduce the yeast by half • When your shaped loaves are rising, you may need to spray the cloth that covers them with water if your kitchen is really dry, to stop the dough from drying out and crusting on top • Bake your bread for a little less time (2–3 minutes less), or it will dry out
Hot, humid, thundery, cloudy If there is too much moisture in the air, the dough, in extreme cases, can become "sweaty" and won't bond properly with the water, making it overly sticky and reluctant to form properly.	• Use 15–20g (about 1–1½ tablespoons) less water • Reduce the yeast by half • Bake your bread for a little longer (around 2–3 minutes longer)
Hot and raining	Same as above
Cold and dry In cold conditions, unless you warm up your water a little, the dough will seal and take a long time to activate—in extreme temperatures it will become dormant and you run the risk of your bread turning out like a brick.	• Use tepid water • Make sure you have a nice warm place for the dough to rise • Cover your dough well with several baking cloths as it rises
Cold outside, central heating on inside Provided the kitchen is at 22–24°C/72–75°F, follow your recipe as usual.	
Cold and wet	Same as above
Snow and ice	Stay in bed!

2

SLOW

Now I want to introduce you to some slower doughs and techniques based on principles that are as old as breadmaking itself. These recipes show you how you can enhance and strengthen your dough with various kinds of "ferment," and then allow it to rise very slowly, so that it builds up a wonderful depth of flavor and gives your baked bread a beautiful texture and crust.

SOURDOUGH & OTHER TYPES OF FERMENTATION

A "ferment" can be used as a base for your dough to develop more slowly, giving a deeper, more complex flavor to the finished loaf.

The idea of using a ferment can be as simple as a piece of dough which you keep back when you make a batch of bread, leave for 4–6 hours at ambient temperature or overnight in the fridge to ferment, then mix with flour, water, and salt to make your next batch of dough (see page 53). Or it can be more complex, as in that Holy Grail of bread, sourdough. It is strange, isn't it, how sourdough has become so fashionable when the technique is one of the oldest ways of making bread in the world? But then throughout the food world there is a feeling of wanting to get back to our roots, of rediscovering the way to grow and rear our food naturally, of appreciating flavors unadulterated by industrial processes. And because sourdough uses wild, rather than commercial, yeast it rightly takes its place up there on the pedestal, as the epitome of natural, flavorsome food.

Flavorwise, what makes sourdough special is that, like a brilliant dish, all the taste and texture sensations come together as one, yet every mouthful can bring a different experience, from the crunchy caramelly crust, through to salty and sweet as well as the characteristic sour notes.

Sourdough is also more digestible than many other types of bread. Its naturally thick crust forces us to chew and get the saliva going, to start breaking down the carbohydrates, a process aided by the sour/vinegary element. As the carbohydrates and proteins are broken down, active "friendly" bacteria are produced, helping to keep the balance of flora in the gastrointestinal tract, on which good digestion depends. These friendly bacteria are similar to those found in plain yogurt—the ones that big companies eliminated for years through heat treatments (to prolong shelf life), but which they are now putting back in, calling them probiotics and charging you extra for them.

Instinctively, we seem to have always known that we need an element of sour to provide balance in our diet. Look at the traditional pairings of foods in most cultures, pre-dating modern fast food, and you can see how we have traditionally put pickles with cheese in a "Ploughman's Lunch" (see page 150), sprinkled vinegar on fish and chips, drunk red wine with pasta in Italy, or paired cornichons (gherkins) with charcuterie and pâté in France.

Fashionable it may be, but there is a lot of confusion about what sourdough actually is. The mere mention of the word is like opening up a Pandora's Box—so many questions. The more people ask me about it, the more I

realize that there is an idea out there that sourdough is the name of a specific bread, whereas in fact it is just a way of describing a process of making bread using the natural fermentation of the wild yeasts that are all around us in everyday ingredients, rather than using commercial yeast. The yeasts are encouraged to grow and ferment over a few days, developing the 'sour' flavor. Think of it as a process similar to the one that happens during cheesemaking.

This use of natural yeasts is the oldest way of fermenting bread. The story goes that back in around 2,000 B.C., a woman by the Nile was making primitive dough for flatbread. She baked most of it, presumably on some kind of hot stone, but left some of the dough behind. The next day she returned, and mixed it into the new dough she was making. When the bread was baked, it was bigger and lighter and that, they say, is how sourdough was born.

So much has been written about sourdough and natural fermentation in recipe books, magazines, in Internet blogs, and so on, that I imagine people's eyes glazing over as if they were reading the instructions on a tax return. I'm not saying sourdough doesn't need a bit of understanding and practice, but making it doesn't have to be scary, and the reward for a little bit of patience is wonderful. I can honestly say that after 30-odd years of baking, I never take a sourdough out of the oven without feeling a real sense of achievement. Any kind of baking gives me immense satisfaction, but the nature of making sourdough never seems short of miraculous.

What I want to do here is show you the way I do *my*

sourdough, because everyone's version is different. You could give the same amount of flour and the same recipe to 10 different bakers and they would produce 10 loaves each with a different character personal to them. People sometimes ask me how to make San Francisco sourdough, because some say the particular, famous bread made in San Francisco is the best in the world, thanks to the special nature of the local wild yeast (cultures are now being distributed all over the world by various enterprising companies). However, I firmly believe that a sourdough will always reflect the environment in which it is being made. I can only tell you how I make my sourdough—call it Bath Sourdough if you like—because the bread I make now may be subtly different to the bread I made following the same technique when I lived in London, or in France. Think about it—the very nature of using natural yeasts depends on the particularity of the ingredients and the peculiarity of the local air. So your sourdough will always truly be your own, representative of you and where you live. Mine is so personal to me, I feel confident I could recognize it in a blind tasting.

In the recipe for my sourdough that follows, I'll take you through the steps slowly and without complicating the issue as if you were in the kitchen with me. I can't promise you your first sourdough will be perfect. It takes a little time and patience—but as surely as anyone can guarantee anything in the world of baking, I can tell you that with a little practice, you will end up with a gorgeous-looking loaf, one that will make you very proud.

MAKING SOURDOUGH

There are lots of different names for the ferment that is at the heart of sourdough bread—levain, biga, starter—but I'm going to stick with that one word: ferment.

The ferment

You can make the simplest and most basic ferment by mixing some warm water with very good, white bread flour and leaving it in a warm place for 36 hours until it starts to ferment. Anything else you add, over and above flour and water, as long as it is live, like yogurt, or sweet and sugary, like honey or fruit, will feed the wild yeast, boost the fermentation, and bolster up the flavor even more. Every bakery will have its own special—often "secret"—recipe and sometimes a particular ingredient will find itself in fashion. Someone will say yogurt is fantastic, or grapes, or raisins macerated in orange juice, and suddenly that is what everyone is using. I like to add a little, very good-quality, local organic honey to get things started.

You also have to consider just how sour you like your sourdough. Some people think it should be blow-your-head-off sour and sharp, whereas personally I prefer a slightly sweeter edge to the dough, so I don't let my ferment ripen too much—that is, I don't leave it as long as other people do before using it.

As I have said, it is important to have a good volume of ferment as the larger the volume, the more you can get the fermentation going. So the recipe overleaf makes enough to use for 2 big loaves and still have some left over to keep going in the fridge for the next time you want to bake (see Refreshing your ferment, page 52).

Another important point is not to spray your kitchen surfaces with antibacterial cleaner just before you start. Of course, good hygiene is always important when you are working with food, but remember that to make a sourdough ferment you are relying on the wild yeasts that are in the air all around you. If you blitz your work surfaces (I've seen people do it) with something that is guaranteed to kill virtually all known germs, and then start your ferment, the wild yeasts won't survive.

And finally, remember that the first time you make sourdough, you need to allow yourself plenty of time, because the whole process will span several days. The silver lining is that once you have made your first batch of ferment, you can keep it going indefinitely, and make bread with it every 2–3 days if you want to.

Stage 1

You will need

50g (1³/4 oz.) spelt flour
  (about ¹/3 cup)
150g (5¹/2 oz.) white bread
  flour (about 1 cup plus
  1¹/2 tbsp.)
20g (²/3 oz.) good honey
150g warm water (about
  ³/4 cup)

To make

● Put all the ingredients into a large bowl (1) and mix very well until you have a softish dough (2). Cut open a large plastic freezer bag and use it to cover the bowl, securing it with an elastic band.

● Leave in a warm place (around 30°C/86°F) for around 36–48 hours until the "dough" has loosened up and smells strongly alcoholic. Avoid the temptation to keep disturbing it. After this time, it will have darkened a bit on the top and bubbles will begin to appear, which will pop slowly (3). This are signs that fermentation has started—that is, you are beginning to grow your own yeast— and you are ready to move on to Stage 2, which involves "feeding" the mixture to help the yeast cells multiply and expand.

Stage 2

You will need

all of your mixture from Stage 1
30g (1 oz.) spelt flour (about
   3¹/₂ tbsp.)
280g (10 oz.) white bread
   flour (about 2 cups)
150g warm water (about
   ³/₄ cup)

To make

● Combine the flours and add
them, along with the water, to the
fermenting mixture in your bowl
(4). Mix well (5). Put the same piece
of plastic back over the top and
secure it with the elastic band,
as before.

● Leave it for 24 hours, in the same
warm place (make sure the temperature doesn't go below 24°C/
75°F or you may stall the fermentation), until the mixture has
developed and expanded a little,
and is starting to smell sweet and
lightly fermented. Now you are
ready to move on to Stage 3.

● For the next stage, you only need
to work with 200g (7 ounces) of
your mixture.

However, don't be tempted to throw
the rest away, since it can be dried,
turned into granules, and stored in
a jar to use another time (see
Making a dry sourdough, page 51).

6

7

8

Stage 3

You will need

200g (7oz.) of your mixture from Stage 2 (reserve the rest, see opposite)

400g (14oz.) white bread flour (about 3 cups)

200g warm water (a scant cup)

To make

● Keeping your 200g (7oz.) of mixture in the bowl you have been using all along (6), add the rest of the ingredients and mix (7) until you have a thick dough (8). Cover with plastic, as before, and leave for 12 hours at no less than 24°C/75°F. At the end of this time, the dough will have started to rise and you can move on to Stage 4, the final stage.

Stage 4

Now that the dough is beginning to rise, you want to slow down the fermentation a little, so that the dough can mature gently. To do this, put it in the bottom of the fridge for another 2 days. If you like your sourdough more sour than sweet (personally, I don't) you can leave it for 4 to 5 days.

You can tell that the ferment is ready to use because, if you pull back a little of the skin that will have formed on top, it will be buttery colored and full of bubbles underneath, like honeycomb (9). It should feel alive and quite sticky, and have a distinctive, slightly acidic and alcoholic smell. If you taste a bit, it will be pleasantly acidic, but not too strong.

You should now have 800g (28oz.) of ferment. Take out half of

it to make your loaves (see page 54), and leave the other half in the bowl. Put the bowl back in the fridge and remember to refresh it every 2–3 days in order to keep it going (see page 52).

9

Making a dry sourdough ferment

If you like, at the end of stage 2, you can take the 600g (21oz.) or so of the mixture you no longer need (see page 49) and dry it for later use. Mix in 500g (18oz.) of white bread flour—it will be really stiff and difficult to mix, but keep at it.

Have a baking tray ready, lined with baking parchment, and put the oven on to 30–40°C/86–104°F or the lowest possible setting.

Cut or shred the mixture into small pieces, the smaller the better, and spread them over the tray. Put the tray into the oven for 2–3 hours until the pieces have dried out. Let cool.

Place the cooled pieces into a food processor and blitz until you have fine granules. These can be stored in an airtight jar for using at a later date.

To re-activate the granules, put them in another jar, add an equal weight of warm water—e.g. 100g granules to 100g water—put the lid on and shake really well. Then put the jar somewhere warm (not less than 25°C/77°F)—near a radiator usually works well—and after a day or two the mixture will start to re-activate. You will see the bubbles forming. At this point, add the same weight of white bread flour (i.e. 100g), and half the weight of water (i.e. 50g), and leave it again. After 24 hours, your mixture should have the same honey-comb texture as the ferment at the end of Stage 4 (see 9 opposite), and you can use it in the same way.

REFRESHING YOUR FERMENT

The beauty of sourdough is that once you have made your initial ferment, you can use some to make your bread, and then keep back a portion of it to use later—provided you keep refreshing it every few days.

The reason you have to keep nourishing your ferment is to keep it alive; if you leave it alone, it will have nothing to feed on and will start feeding off itself, eventually turning rotten and dying.

To refresh your ferment, the rule of thumb is to weigh it, then mix it with an equal weight of water and double the weight of white bread flour. So, to the 400g (14oz.) of ferment you have kept back after following Stages 1–4 on pages 48–50, add 400g (about 2 cups) of water and 800g (about 6 cups) of white bread flour. Mix into a quite firm dough, cover your bowl with a large, split freezer bag, and secure it with an elastic band. Leave the ferment in the fridge for 2–3 days, during which time it will continue to ferment and expand very slowly, ready for your next baking session. If you need to use it sooner, take it out of the fridge and leave it at room temperature for a few hours.

If you are not going to bake another batch for a while, remember you will need to keep refreshing your ferment every 2–3 days. Bear in mind that it will keep expanding, so unless you want your fridge to be over-run with it, just keep back 400g of ferment each time, and discard the rest.

One of the things people ask me all the time is how should their ferment look? Well, unfortunately, there is no standard appearance, no equivalent of a paint chart that will tell you the precise color, because we are dealing with some-thing that is living and changing.

My usual response is that as long as you can see signs of fermentation and there is no indication that the ferment is going rotten, it is OK. That means it should smell pleasantly acidic and alcoholic, and if you peel back a bit of the skin on top, you should see that stringy, honeycomb texture that I described at the end of Stage 4 on page 50.

If at any point you feel the ferment is becoming too hard, dense, and dormant, and is losing its smell, it is probably too cold for it to be properly active. Simply take it out of the fridge for 4 hours or so to give it time to come back

to life, and then put it back into the fridge again.

If the ferment starts to smell too pungent, over-ripe, and vinegary, and if there is a wateriness about the texture, this is a sign that it is on the turn. To remedy the situation, simply scrape off and discard the top to reveal the nice, pleasantly smelling honeycomb center. Weigh that, and refresh it as usual by mixing it with an equal weight of water and double the weight of flour. Put it back in the fridge and you should be back on track.

I know this all may sound complicated the first time you make a ferment, but you will soon get the hang of seeing what is going on, and keeping your ferment ticking over nicely—taking it out of the fridge for a while if it gets too dormant, or removing the top and starting again with the heart of the ferment if it tries to race ahead.

Keeping your ferment going when you are away

No, you don't need to take your ferment with you on vacation! You can keep it going in the fridge in your absence. The key is to get a good volume of it going before you leave. The larger the quantity, the slower it will mature and the longer it can go before you need to feed it again.

What I do is this. For a few weeks before I go away, instead of keeping only 400g (14oz.) of ferment to refresh each time, I don't throw any of it away. Instead, I weigh what is in the fridge, mix in the same weight of water and double the weight of flour and keep repeating that every few days, so that I build up the quantity of ferment to about 2kg (about 4½lb.). That will happily keep for a few weeks in the fridge while I am away, and then, when I come back, I take off the top, leaving myself with 400g (14oz.) at the heart of the ferment. I refresh this, as usual, with 400g (about 2 cups) of water and 800g (about 6 cups) of flour, and then get back into the normal routine of refreshing 400g (14oz.) of it (discarding the rest) every 2–3 days.

MAKING YOUR SOURDOUGH BREAD

Now you are ready to make your loaves. You need 400g (14oz.) of ferment (half the quantity you have made) for this recipe. Keep the rest and refresh it (see page 52, Refreshing your ferment). Remember that sourdough takes a long time to rise, so the dough you make today won't actually go into the oven until tomorrow.

Preparation: Ferment + 30 minutes   **Resting:** 2 hours   **2nd Rising:** 17–19 hours   **Baking:** 30–45 minutes
Freezing: Freezes well fully baked. Defrost at room temperature.

In this and some of the other breads in the book I keep the salt and only add it halfway through working the dough. Salt slows the action of yeast so delaying its addition gives the wild yeast a chance to develop first.

Makes 2 large loaves

You will need

90g (3oz.) spelt flour (about 2/3 cup)
700g (25oz.) white bread flour (about 51/4 cups)
400g (14oz.) ferment (see Stages 1–4,
   pages 48–50)
650g water (about 31/4 cups)
20g (2/3oz.) salt (about 4 level tsp.)
fine spelt or white flour for dusting, plus a little
   fine semolina, for dusting the peels

To prepare

Have ready 2 wicker bread-rising baskets or 2 bowls lined with baking cloths. You will also need 2 quite large wooden peels or upturned baking trays for transferring the loaves to the oven.

To make

● Combine the flours in your large mixing bowl. Add your ferment, ripping it into pieces (1) and mixing it into the flour at the same time.

● Add the water (2) and mix together, using your scraper (3). When everything starts to come together into a dough, use your scraper to turn it out onto your work surface (don't flour the work surface first) (4).

● Start to work the dough (see pages 24–6). After about 10 minutes, sprinkle the salt over the top (5) and continue to work (6) until the dough is smooth, strong, and elastic, and comes away from your work surface cleanly (7).

● Lightly flour your work surface, and then form the dough into a ball (see page 27) (8–9). Put back into your (lightly floured) mixing bowl, cover with a baking cloth and let it rest for 1 hour (see page 28).

• Lightly flour your surface, turn out the dough with the help of your scraper, fold it (see page 28) and put it back into your bowl. Let it rest for another hour.

• Lightly flour your surface, turn the dough out and divide it into 2 equal pieces (about 900g (2lb.) each).

• Form each piece into a ball (see page 27).

• Dust your bread-rising baskets or cloth-lined bowls really well with either spelt or white flour. (One of the characteristics of sourdough when it has been baked is the contrast of the dark burst against the white, floured crust, so you do need to flour your baskets or bowls very well at this stage.)

• Put your balls of dough, seam-side up, into your floured baskets or bowls (10)—the smooth side of the dough that is nestling in the bowl, covering itself in flour, will eventually become the top of your bread.

10

• Now you need to let the dough rise for 16–18 hours. This needs to happen fairly slowly at this point, so leave it in a slightly cooler place than you would normally (17–18°C/62–64°F is the ideal temperature).

• Preheat your oven to 250°C/500°F roughly 2 hours before you want to bake. Remember to put in your baking stones or pans to get hot, one on each shelf of your oven if you're going to bake both loaves at the same time.

Lightly dust your wooden peels or upturned baking trays with fine semolina.

• After about 16–18 hours, the dough should have doubled in size and be springy to the touch (11). If it hasn't risen enough, leave it for an hour or so longer.

• Turn out each ball of dough onto a lightly floured (12) wooden peel or flat baking tray (13) so that the rounded side of each loaf is upwards (14). They should be coated in flour from the bread-rising baskets/bowls.

• Slash the top of each loaf with a lame (15) or sharp blade (see page 13 for different ways of doing this).

• Open the oven door and quickly mist the inside of the oven with your water spray—see page 22 (16). Slide your loaves onto the hot baking stones or trays in the oven (17), and spray some more before quickly closing the oven door.

• Set your timer for 5 minutes. After this time, turn down the heat to 220°C/460°F and bake for another 25 minutes (you might need to swap the loaves around halfway through baking, to make sure they are evenly baked). They are ready when the crust, where it has burst open, is pronounced and dark golden brown (18). The bottom should also be dark golden brown and sound hollow if you tap it (19). If they aren't ready, turn the heat down to 210°C for another 10–15 minutes. Cool completely on a rack before eating.

VARIATIONS

Once you have made your ferment, you can make variations on the sourdough recipe by adding some rye or whole-wheat bread flour. Wholemeal makes a more dense bread, great for everyday use, and especially good toasted for breakfast, or with goat cheese—and its healthy credentials appeal to many people. Rye makes a denser bread still, with an earthier flavor, that is good with seafood and charcuterie.

Brown sourdough

Makes 2 large loaves

You will need

400g (14oz.) ferment (see Stages 1–4, page 48–50)

200g (7oz.) white bread flour (about 1¹/₄ cups)

600g (21oz.) whole-wheat bread flour (about 4¹/₂ cups)

680g water (between 3¹/₃ and 3¹/₂ cups)

20g (²/₃oz.) salt (about 4 level tsp.)

whole-wheat bread flour, for dusting, plus a little fine semolina, for dusting the peels

To make

Mix all the ingredients together and make the bread in exactly the same way as for sourdough on pages 54–7. This time, use whole-wheat bread flour for dusting your bread-rising baskets/bowls.

Rye sourdough

Makes 2 large loaves

You will need

400g (14oz.) ferment (see Stages 1–4, pages 48–50)

300g (11oz.) white bread flour (about 2¹/₃ cups)

500g (18oz.) dark rye flour (about 3³/₄ cups)

600g water (about 3 cups)

20g (²/₃oz.) salt (about 4 level tsp.)

rye flour, for dusting, plus a little fine semolina, for dusting the peels

To make

Mix all the ingredients together and make the bread in exactly the same way as for sourdough on pages 54–7. This time, use rye flour for dusting your bread-rising baskets/bowls.

BAGUETTE WITH A POOLISH FERMENT

A poolish is simply a different, more liquid-style of ferment made with fresh yeast. It was introduced into France by Polish bakers, and helps to give a light texture to the dough, develop a sweetness of flavor, and give a good color to the crust.

Preparation: Ferment + 25 minutes **Resting:** $1^1/_2$–$1^3/_4$ hours **2nd Rising:** 1–$1^1/_2$ hours **Baking:** 12–15 minutes for baguettes, 35–40 minutes for large loaf, 20–25 minutes for small loaf **Freezing:** Part bake until the crust just starts to color: about 8–10 minutes for baguettes, 12–25 minutes for small loaves, or 20–25 for large loaves. Finish baking from frozen in a preheated oven at 200°C/400°F for 8–10 minutes for baguettes, 12–15 minutes for small loaves, or 15–18 for large loaves. Cool well as usual.

Makes 10 baguettes, plus 1 large or 2 small loaves

FOR THE POOLISH FERMENT

You will need
5g fresh yeast (1 level tsp.)
350g water (just over $1^1/_2$ cups water)
300g (11oz.) white bread flour (about $2^1/_3$ cups)
50g ($1^3/_4$oz.) dark rye flour (about 6 level tbsp.)

To make
● Stir the yeast into the water in your mixing bowl, then add the flours and mix well with a plastic scraper. Cover with a large, split plastic freezer bag and secure with an elastic band.

● Put into the fridge overnight, or leave at room temperature for 4–5 hours to mature. (I prefer to use the fridge method, since the slower the maturation the better developed the flavor and characteristic crumb and crust of this bread.)

FOR THE BREAD

You will need
all of the poolish
1.3kg (just under 3lb.) white bread flour (about 10 cups)
700g (about $3^1/_2$ cups) water
20g ($^2/_3$oz.) fresh yeast (about 4 level tsp.)
30g (1oz.) salt (about 2 level tbsp.)
a little white or cornmeal flour for dusting, plus a little fine semolina, for dusting the peels

To prepare
Preheat the oven to 250°C/500°F. Unless you are going to bake in batches, you will need to use both shelves of the oven and put in 2 baking stones or baking trays, or one of each, to get good and hot. Again, unless you are baking in batches, you will need enough peels or trays to load all the loaves before putting them into the oven. Line 3 large baking trays with couches or baking cloths.

To make

• Keeping the poolish in its bowl, add the rest of the ingredients, except the salt, and mix together with your scraper. When everything starts to come together into a dough, use your scraper to help you turn it out onto your work surface (don't flour the work surface first).

• Start to work the dough (see pages 24–6). After about 10 minutes, sprinkle the salt onto the dough and continue to work until smooth and elastic.

• Lightly flour the work surface and then form the dough into a ball (see page 27). Put the dough back into your (lightly floured) mixing bowl, cover with a baking cloth and let it rest for 1^1/$_2$ hours (see page 28). Lightly flour your work surface and, with the help of your scraper, turn out the dough.

• Cut off a 2kg (4^1/$_2$lb.) piece and divide into 10 x 200g (7-oz.) pieces (see page 31), cover with a baking cloth and let it rest on your work surface for 15 minutes.

• Shape the remaining piece of dough into 1 large loaf or 2 smaller ones (see page 32), cover and let it rise for 1^1/$_2$ hours on one of the lightly floured couche or cloth-lined trays.

• Shape the baguettes one at a time (see page 35) and place on your lightly floured couche or cloth-lined trays, seam-side down. To prevent them from touching each other, make a pleat in the couche or cloth as you lay each baguette down on the tray. Cover with another baking cloth and let them rise for 1–1^1/$_2$ hours until the baguettes have just under doubled in volume.

• Sprinkle some fine semolina onto your peels, and then place 2 baguettes on each, seam-side down. Slash the tops (see page 37).

• Open the oven door and quickly mist the inside of the oven with your water spray (see page 22). Use the peels to slide the baguettes onto your hot baking stones or trays. You should be able to fit 5 baguettes on each stone or tray; if not, you'll have to bake in batches. Spray the oven before quickly closing the oven door. Bake for 12–15 minutes until the baguettes are golden brown on the top and bottom. Take out and cool on wire racks.

• When the baguettes come out, you can bake your loaves. The large loaf will need around 35–40 minutes; the smaller ones will need 20–25 minutes. Remove from the oven and cool on wire racks.

ALE & YEAST POOLISH

Another bread made with a poolish ferment, this time flavored with ale. Adding the ale, another live ingredient, gives a lively, sweet-sour, beery character to the dough, which results in a creamy, slightly sweet flavored bread, with a fantastic bursting crust. Try a big wedge with a hearty bowl of cassoulet and a glass of red wine (see picture overleaf).

Preparation: Ferment + 20 minutes **Resting:** 2 hours **2nd Rising:** 1–2 hours **Baking:** 25 minutes
Freezing: Part bake until the crust just starts to color: about 8–10 minutes for baguettes, 12–25 minutes for small loaves, or 20–25 for large loaves. Finish baking from frozen in a preheated oven at 200ºC/400ºF for 8–10 minutes for baguettes, 12–15 minutes for small loaves, or 15–18 for large loaves. Cool well as usual.

Makes 4 small loaves

FOR THE POOLISH FERMENT

You will need
125g ale (such as Bass ale or Samual Adams), lukewarm (about $2/3$ cup)
125g ($4^1/2$oz.) white bread flour (a scant cup)
5g fresh yeast (about 1 level tsp.)

To make
Mix all the ingredients together in your mixing bowl. Cover with a large, split plastic freezer bag, secured with an elastic band, and let it rest at room temperature for 3–5 hours until the mixture is well risen and some bubbles appear.

FOR THE BREAD

You will need
all of the poolish
750g (26oz.) white bread flour (about $5^1/2$– $5^3/4$ cups)
50g ($1^3/4$oz.) whole-wheat bread flour (6 level tsp.)
5g fresh yeast (about 1 level tsp.)
500g water (about $2^1/2$ cups)
15g ($1/2$oz.) salt (about 1 level tbsp.)
a little white flour for dusting, plus a little semolina flour, for dusting the peels

To prepare
Preheat the oven to 250ºC/500ºF. Unless you are going to bake in batches, you will need to use both shelves of the oven and put in 2 baking stones or baking trays, or one of each, to get good and hot. Again, unless you are baking in batches, you will need enough peels or trays to load all the loaves before putting them into the oven. Line 2 large trays with couches or baking cloths.

To make

● Keeping the poolish in the same bowl, add all of the ingredients for the bread, except the salt, and mix together with your scraper. When everything starts to come together into a dough, use your scraper to help you turn it out onto your work surface (don't flour it first).

● Start to work the dough (see pages 24–6). After about 10 minutes, sprinkle the salt over the top and continue to work the dough until it is smooth, strong, and elastic, and comes away from your work surface cleanly.

● Lightly flour your work surface, and then form the dough into a ball (see page 27). Put the dough back into your (lightly floured) mixing bowl, cover with a baking cloth, and let it rest for 1 hour (see page 28).

● Lightly flour your work surface again, and turn out the dough with the help of your scraper. Fold the dough (see page 28), and then put it back into the bowl. Cover and let it rest for another hour.

● Again lightly flour your work surface. Turn the dough out of the bowl and divide it into 4 equal pieces of about 400g (14oz.) each (see page 31).

● Shape each piece into a loaf (see page 32) and lay 2 of them on each of your (lightly floured) couche or cloth-lined trays, seam-side down. Cover with a baking cloth and let it rise for 1–2 hours until just under double in volume.

● Dust your peels lightly with a little fine semolina, load the loaves onto your peels, and slash the tops.

● Open the oven door and quickly mist the inside of your oven using your water spray (see page 22). Slide the loaves onto your hot baking stones or trays in the oven—2 on each—and spray some more before quickly closing the door.

● Set the timer for 5 minutes. After this time, turn down the heat to 220ºC/425ºF and bake for another 20 minutes, or until the loaves are dark golden brown and the bottoms sound hollow when tapped.

AUTOLYSE METHOD

This method was developed by Professor Raymond Calvel in France. He discovered that simply by mixing water and flour and letting it rest for anything between 20 minutes and 1 hour, before adding the rest of the ingredients (if using a ferment), the dough would "self-mix" a little, giving you a head start. It won't develop the gluten—to do that you still need to work your dough—but you will find it comes together in a much shorter time.

Preparation: Ferment + 45 minutes **Resting:** $2^{1}/_{4}$ hours **2nd Rising:** 1–$1^{1}/_{2}$ hours **Baking:** 12–15 minutes for baguettes, 35–40 minutes for large loaf, 20–25 minutes for small loaf **Freezing:** Part bake until the crust just starts to color: about 8–10 minutes for baguettes, 12–25 minutes for small loaves, or 20–25 for large loaves. Finish baking from frozen in a preheated oven at 200°C/400°F for 8–10 minutes for baguettes, 12–15 minutes for small loaves or 15–18 for large loaves. Cool well as usual.

Although in the recipe I say to let your bread rise for 1–$1^{1}/_{2}$ hours (as usual, in a warm, draft-free place), this bread is also a good candidate for a slower rising overnight in the fridge (see Retarded bread-rising, page 36). If you try it, you will see that it will enhance the flavor and develop the sugars a bit more, so that you will notice a nice reddish tinge to the crust.

Makes 10 baguettes, plus 1 large loaf
or 2 small ones
You will need
950g ($33^{1}/_{2}$oz.) white bread flour (about
   7–$7^{1}/_{3}$ cups)
50g ($1^{3}/_{4}$oz.) dark rye flour (about 6 level tbsp.)
720g water (about $3^{2}/_{3}$ cups)
300g (11oz.) ferment (see Stages 1–4, pages 48–50) or fermented white dough (see page 73)
10g ($^{1}/_{3}$oz.) fresh yeast (about 2 level tsp.)
20g ($^{2}/_{3}$oz.) salt (about 4 level tsp.)
a little white flour for dusting, plus a little semolina
   flour, for dusting the peels

To prepare
Preheat the oven to 250°C/500°F. Unless you are going to bake in batches, you will need to use both shelves of the oven and put in 2 baking stones or baking trays, or one of each, to get good and hot.

Unless you are baking in batches, you will need enough peels or trays to load all the loaves before putting them into the oven. Line 3 large baking trays with couches or baking cloths.

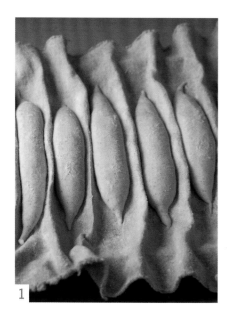  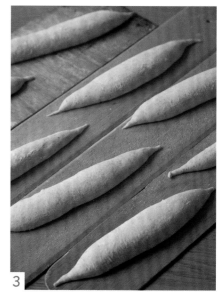

To make

● Mix the flours with the water in your mixing bowl. Cover with a large, split plastic freezer bag, secured with an elastic band, and let rest for 30 minutes.

● Add the ferment and yeast and mix together, using your scraper. When everything starts to come together into a dough, use your scraper to help you turn it out onto your work surface (don't flour it first).

● Work the dough (see pages 24–6) until it starts to become smooth and elastic. Sprinkle the salt over it and work it for another 2–3 minutes.

● Lightly flour your work surface, and then form the dough into a ball (see page 27). Put back into your (lightly floured) mixing bowl, cover with a baking cloth and let it rest for 1 hour.

● Lightly flour your work surface again, turn out the dough with the help of your scraper, fold the dough a few times (see page 28) then put it back into your (lightly floured) bowl. Cover with a baking cloth and let it rest for another 30 minutes.

● Lightly flour your surface again, turn out the dough and cut off 2kg (4½lb.) piece. Divide it into 10 x 200g (7-ounce) pieces (see page 31). Cover and leave out on your work surface to rest for 15 minutes.

● Shape the remaining piece of dough into 1 large loaf or 2 smaller ones (see page 32) and let it rise for 1–1½ hours on a lightly floured couche or cloth-lined trays.

● Shape the baguettes (see page 35) and place them on your lightly floured couche or cloth-lined trays, seam-side down. To keep them separate, make a pleat in the couche or cloth as you lay each baguette down on the tray (1). Cover with another baking cloth and let rise for 1–1½ hours until just under double in volume. Alternatively, follow the instructions for Retarded bread-rising on page 36.

● Sprinkle a little fine semolina onto your peels and place 2 baguettes on each, seam-side down (2–3). Slash the tops (see page 37) (4).

● Open the oven door and quickly mist the inside of the oven with your water spray (see page 22). Use the peels to slide your baguettes onto the hot baking stones or trays (5). You should be able to get 5 on each, but if not, bake in batches. Spray the oven again a couple more times, then quickly close the oven door. Bake for 12–15 minutes until the baguettes are golden brown on the top and bottom (6). Take out and cool on a wire tray.

● When the baguettes come out, you can bake your loaves. The large loaf will need 35–40 minutes; smaller ones around 20–25 minutes. Cool on wire racks.

BAGUETTES WITH FERMENTED DOUGH

This bread uses an all-purpose white dough suitable for loaves, baguettes, and rolls, etc. Fill a baguette with some good ham and grainy mustard and you have a delicious lunch. Once the ingredients are mixed, you can work it, shape it, and bake it as usual. However, you can also leave it to ferment for 6 hours at ambient room temperature or, better still, overnight in the fridge or a very cool place, and use it as a slightly different kind of ferment on which to build your loaf. Lighter than a poolish ferment, it will give you bread that is slightly darker looking, with a more rustic feel about it and a lovely depth of flavor.

Preparation: Ferment + 15 minutes   **Resting:** 3 hours   **2nd Rising:** 1 hour   **Baking:** 12–15 minutes

Makes 12 baguettes

FOR THE FERMENTED WHITE DOUGH
You will need
10g (^{1}/$_3$oz.) fresh yeast (about 2 level tsp.)
500g (about 18oz.) white bread flour (about
   3^3/$_4$ cups)
10g (^{1}/$_3$oz.) salt (about 2 level tsp.)
350g water (about 1^3/$_4$ cups)

This will make around 900g (2lb.) dough. You only need 600g (21oz.) for this recipe, so you can leave the rest in the fridge for a few days and use in your next batch of baking. Alternatively, you could use it as a pizza base, or to make the Flamiche on page 112.

To make
● Rub the yeast into the flour using your fingertips, add the salt and the water and mix well until the dough begins to come together. Turn out onto your (unfloured) work surface and work the dough (see pages 24-6).

● Return the dough to your (lightly floured) mixing bowl.

Cover with a baking cloth and let it rest at room temperature for 6 hours, or overnight in the fridge (or for up to 48 hours) until it has doubled in volume.

FOR THE BREAD
You will need
950g (33^1/$_2$oz.) white bread flour (about 7–7^1/$_3$ cups)
50g (1^3/$_4$oz.) dark rye flour (about 6 level tbsp.)
720g water (about 3^2/$_3$ cups)
600g (21oz.) fermented white dough
20g (^{2}/$_3$oz.) salt (about 4^1/$_2$ level tsp.)
white flour for dusting, plus a little fine semolina,
   for dusting the peels

To prepare
Preheat your oven to 250ºC/500ºF. Unless you are going to bake in batches, you will need to use both shelves of the oven and put in 2 baking stones or baking trays, or one of each, to get good and hot.

   Unless you are baking in batches, you will need enough peels or trays to load all the loaves before putting them into the oven. Line 2 large baking trays with couches or baking cloths.

To make

- Mix the 2 flours in a large mixing bowl, and then stir in the water. Mix well until the dough comes together. Cover with a baking cloth and let rest for 30 minutes.

- Add the fermented dough and mix well. When everything starts to come together, use your scraper to help you turn the dough out onto your work surface (don't flour it first).

- Work the dough (see pages 24-6) until it starts to become smooth and elastic. Sprinkle the salt on it and work it for another 2–3 minutes.

- Lightly flour your work surface, and then fold the dough into a ball (see page 27). Put the dough back into your (lightly floured) mixing bowl, cover with a baking cloth and let it rest for $1^1/2$ hours (see page 28).

- Lightly flour your work surface, turn out the dough with the help of your scraper, fold (see page 28), and put back into the bowl. Let it rest for another hour.

- Lightly flour your work surface again, and turn out the dough. Divide it into 12 x 185g ($6^1/2$-oz.) pieces (see page 31) and cover with a baking cloth to stop them from drying out while you're shaping them.

- Shape the first baguette (see page 35) and place on a (lightly floured) couche or cloth-lined tray, seam-side down. Make a pleat in the couche or cloth, then shape the next baguette and lay it on the tray, so that the pleat keeps it separate from the first one. Continue forming your baguettes and pleating the couche/cloth so that none of the loaves touch each other. Cover with another baking cloth and let them rise for about 1 hour, or until just double in volume.

- Sprinkle some fine semolina onto your peels and place 2 baguettes on each, seam-side down. Slash the tops (see page 37).

- Open the oven door and quickly mist the inside of the oven with your water spray (see page 22). Use the peels to slide your baguettes onto the hot baking stones or trays in the oven. You should be able to fit 6 baguettes on each. Spray some more before quickly closing the oven door. Bake for 12–15 minutes until golden brown. Remove from the oven and cool on wire racks.

THE BERTINET KITCHEN
cooking learning eating
TELEPHONE: 01225 445531

3

DIFFERENT

This chapter is simply a collection of breads that I enjoy making, using different ideas and some of the fascinating, sometimes unusual, flours that I am continually discovering from around the world. Some give you a chance to experiment with the ferments and methods that I explained in the previous chapter, but there are also breads that are quick to make, as well as some recipes, like those for pretzels, blinis, and bagels, that use different techniques.

SEEDED BREAD

You can make up your own mix of favourite edible seeds, from sunflower to pumpkin or fennel, use a prepared mix, or combine seeds and rolled oats. You can also buy good strong bread flour that already has a mixture of seeds in it (page 16). If you decide to use this, just substitute 1kg (2¼ lb.) seeded flour for all the flours and seeds in the list of ingredients below.

Preparation: ferment + 25 minutes **Resting:** 1½ hours **2nd Rising:** 1½ hours **Baking:** 33–38 minutes
Freezing: Freezes well fully baked. Defrost at room temperature

Makes 3 large loaves

You will need
300g (11oz.) fermented white dough (see page 73)
700g (25oz.) strong white bread flour
100g (3½oz.) fine cornmeal (about ⅔ cup)
50g (1¾oz.) rye flour (about 6 tbsp.)
150g (5⅓oz.) whole-wheat flour (about 1 cup
    plus 2 tbsp.)
250g (8oz.) seed blend (about 2 cups)
30g (1oz.) dark brown sugar (about 2½ tbsp.)
20g (⅔oz.) salt (about 4 level tsp.)
20g (⅔oz.) fresh yeast (about 4 level tsp.)
700g water (about 3½ cups)
white flour, for dusting
extra seeds or rolled oats (optional)
a little butter or vegetable oil for tins

To prepare
Lightly grease 3 x 800g loaf pans. Preheat the oven to 250°C.

To make
● Combine all of the ingredients in your mixing bowl, using your scraper. When everything starts to come together into a dough, use your scraper to help you turn it out onto your work surface (don't flour it first). Work the dough (see pages 24–6).

● Lightly flour your work surface, and then form the dough into a ball (see page 27). Put it back into your (lightly floured) mixing bowl, cover with a baking cloth and let it rest for 45 minutes.

● Lightly flour your surface again, turn out the dough, fold (see page 28), and form back into a ball. Put back into your (lightly floured) bowl and let rest, covered, for 45 minutes.

● Lightly flour your work surface again, and divide your dough into 3 pieces (see page 31). Shape into loaves (see page 32) and, if you like, roll the tops lightly in some seeds or oats. Put into your greased pans. Cover with baking cloths and let rise for 1½ hours.

● Open the oven door and quickly mist the inside of your oven with your water spray (see page 22). Slide in your loaves, and spray some more before quickly closing the door.

● Set your timer for 3 minutes. After this time, turn down the heat to 220°C/425°F and bake for another 30–35 minutes. Remove the loaves from the pans and tap the bottoms, if they don't sound hollow pop them back in for a few minutes. Turn them out and cool on wire racks.

SPELT BREAD

Spelt is enjoying a real renaissance, and is especially valuable for those who have an intolerance to wheat. I particularly like it toasted, with cheese, or with seafood.

Preparation: ferment + 30 minutes **Resting:** 1¹/₂ hours **2nd Rising:** 1 hour **Baking:** 30–35 minutes

Makes 2 large loaves
FOR THE POOLISH
You will need
500g (18oz.) spelt flour (about 3³/₄ cups)
500g water (about 2¹/₂ cups)
10g (¹/₃oz.) fresh yeast (about 2 level tsp.)

To make
Mix everything together in your mixing bowl, cover with a baking cloth or large split freezer bag secured with an elastic band, and let it rest for 3–5 hours in a warm place, or overnight in the fridge.

FOR THE BREAD
You will need
all of the poolish
500g (18oz.) spelt flour (about 3³/₄ cups)
10g (¹/₃oz.) fresh yeast (about 2 level tsp.)
20g (²/₃oz.) salt (about 4 level tsp.)
150g water (about ³/₄ cup)
100g (3¹/₂oz.) whole spelt grains, soak them
   overnight in warm water (optional)
a little butter or vegetable oil for pans, if using
spelt flour, for dusting, plus a little fine semolina,
   for dusting the peels

To prepare
Preheat the oven to 250°C/500°F. Unless baking in pans, put in 2 baking stones or trays to get good and hot. Either lightly grease 2 x 800g (28oz.) bread pans or have ready 2 bread-rising baskets or bowls lined with baking cloths. Unless you are using pans, you will also need a peel or tray to load the loaves into the oven.

To make
● Combine the poolish with the rest of the ingredients and mix together with the help of your scraper. Use your scraper to help you turn out the dough onto your work surface (don't flour it first). Work the dough (see pages 24–6) until it is smooth and elastic.

● Lightly flour your work surface, and then form the dough into a ball (see page 27). Put it back into your (lightly floured) mixing bowl, cover with a baking cloth, and let it rest for 1 hour.

● Lightly flour your work surface again, turn out the dough, and cut it in half, using the sharp edge of your scraper. Cover with baking cloths and let rest on the work surface for 15 minutes.

● Either shape into 2 large loaves (see page 32) and put into your greased pans, or form into balls and put into your (lightly floured) bread-rising baskets or cloth-lined bowls. Cover with baking cloths and let rise for 1 hour, or until just under double in volume, then turn the loaves in the baskets over onto a peel ready for baking.

● Open the oven door and quickly mist the inside of the oven with your water spray. Put in your pans, or slide the loaves onto your hot baking stones or trays in the oven, and spray again before quickly closing the oven door. Set your timer for 2 minutes. After this time, turn down the heat to 220°C/425°F and bake for another 25–30 minutes, until the bottom of each loaf sounds hollow when tapped. Cool on wire racks.

DARK RYE BREAD WITH RAISINS

You can omit the raisins if you prefer, like the loaves overleaf (to make these follow the shaping and baking method on page 73, Bread with Fermented Dough). Personally I enjoy the sweetness the raisins add, and I like to serve this bread with cheese and chutney, or even alongside a curry which contains fruit. The addition of the fermented white dough helps to develop the gluten in the dough, strengthening it, and making the finished bread lighter than rye can sometimes be.

Preparation: Ferment + 25 minutes   **Resting:** 2 hours   **2nd Rising:** $1^{1}/_{2}$ hours   **Baking:** 1 hour
Freezing: Freezes well fully baked. Defrost at room temperature.

Makes 4 small loaves

You will need
1kg ($2^{1}/_{4}$lb.) dark rye flour (about $7^{1}/_{3}$–$7^{2}/_{3}$ cups)
500g (18oz.) fermented white dough (see page 73)
25g (about 1oz.) fresh yeast (about 5 level tsp.)
20g ($^{2}/_{3}$oz.) salt (about 4 level tsp.)
750g water (about $3^{3}/_{4}$ cups)
1 teaspoon caraway seeds
2 teaspoons ground coffee (proper coffee not instant!)
400g (14oz.) raisins (about $2^{3}/_{4}$ cups)
a little fine semolina, for dusting (optional)
a little butter or vegetable oil for pans

To prepare
Lightly grease 4 x 400g (14oz.) bread pans or have ready 4 bread-rising baskets or bowls lined with baking cloths. (I have some unlined rush bread-rising baskets from Brittany that I like to use for this bread.)

Preheat the oven to 250°C/500°F. Unless you are going to bake in batches, you will need to use both shelves of the oven and, unless baking in pans, put in 2 baking stones or baking trays, or one of each, to get good and hot.

Also, unless you are using pans, you will need enough peels or trays to load the loaves before putting them into the oven.

To make
● Combine all the ingredients except the raisins in a mixing bowl with the help of your scraper. The dough will feel extra sticky, but this is normal. Use your scraper to turn it out onto your work surface (don't flour it first).

● Work the dough (see pages 24–6) for 8–10 minutes, then add the raisins and continue to work until the dough is smooth and the raisins are all incorporated.

● Lightly flour your work surface, and then form the dough into a ball (see page 27). Put it back into your (lightly floured) mixing bowl, cover with a baking cloth, and let it rest for 1 hour.

● Lightly flour your work surface, turn out the dough, fold (see page 28), then form it into a ball and once more put back into the bowl. Cover with your baking cloth and let it rest for another hour.

● Lightly flour your work surface, turn out the dough and divide into 4 x 650g (23oz.) pieces (see page 31)—650g (23oz.) of this dough will fit into a 400g (14oz.) pan, as it is quite tight and won't rise up as much as other doughs. Either shape each piece into a log-shaped loaf and put into your prepared pan (see page 32), or form into a ball and put into your (lightly floured) bread-rising basket or cloth-lined bowl. Cover with more baking cloths and let rise for 1¹/₂ hours.

● If you're not using pans, sprinkle some semolina onto your peels or trays and then place the loaves on top, seam-side down. Slash the tops (see page 37)—you don't need to slash the tops of loaves in pans.

● Open the oven door and quickly mist the inside of the oven with your water spray (see page 22). Put in your pans, or slide the loaves onto your hot baking stones or trays in the oven, and spray some more before quickly closing the oven door.

● Set your timer for 5 minutes. After this time, turn down the heat to 210°C/400°F and bake for about 1 hour until the bottom of each loaf sounds hollow when tapped. Cool on wire racks. This is very compact bread, so you will need to allow several hours for the loaves to cool down completely.

BRETON BREAD

The salt I use for this recipe is sel-gris from Brittany—as its name suggests, it looks quite gray and has a minerally taste. You need to dissolve it in a little of the water from the recipe before using, because it is quite coarse.

Preparation: Ferment + 30 minutes **Resting:** $1^1/_2$ hours **2nd Rising:** $1^1/_2$–2 hours **Baking:** 20–25 minutes
Freezing: Freezes well fully baked. Defrost at room temperature.

Makes 2 large loaves

You will need
15g ($^1/_2$oz.) sel-gris (about $2^1/_4$ tsp.)
700g water (about $3^1/_2$ cups)
750g (26oz.) white bread flour (about
    $5^1/_2$ –$5^3/_4$ cups)
200g (7oz.) buckwheat flour (about $1^1/_2$ cups)
50g ($1^3/_4$oz.) dark rye flour (about 6 tbsp.)
300g (11oz.) fermented white dough (see page 73)
10g ($^1/_3$oz.) fresh yeast (about 2 level tsp.)
a little white flour for dusting, plus a little fine
    semolina, for dusting the peels

To prepare
Preheat the oven to 250°C/500°F and put in 2 baking stones or baking trays, or one of each, to get good and hot. You will need 2 bread-rising baskets or bowls lined with baking cloths, and 2 peels or trays to load the loaves before putting them into the oven.

To make
● Dissolve the salt in a little of the water and stir until the grains have disappeared. Add to all the other ingrdients and mix together in a mixing bowl, using your scraper. When everything starts to come together into a dough, use your scraper to help you turn it out onto your work surface (don't flour it first). Work the dough (see pages 24–6).

● Lightly flour your work surface, and then form the dough into a ball (see page 27). Put it back into your (lightly floured) mixing bowl, cover with a thick baking cloth, and let it rest for 45 minutes.

● Lightly flour your work surface again, turn out the dough, and fold (see page 28). Form it into a ball once more and put it back into the bowl. Let it rest for another 45 minutes.

● Cut the dough in half with your scraper and shape into 2 round loaves, following the technique for forming into a ball on page 27. Flour your bread-rising baskets well, put a ball of dough in each, cover with a baking cloth, and let rise for $1^1/_2$–2 hours until just under double in volume.

● Dust your peels or trays with a little fine semolina and turn out a ball of dough onto each. Slash the top of each loaf with a lame or sharp blade (see page 37). Open the oven door and quickly mist the inside of the oven with your water spray. Use the peels to slide the loaves onto your hot baking stones or trays, spray some more before quickly closing the oven door.

● Set your timer for 5 minutes. After this time, turn down the heat to 210°C/400°F and bake for another 15–20 minutes, until they are dark golden on top and sound hollow when tapped underneath. Let cool on a wire rack.

CABERNET GRAPE FLOUR BREAD

This is a really unusual bread which uses flour made from grape skins. In Canada, where it is produced, chefs are experimenting with it, not only in bread, but in pasta and biscuits, too.

Preparation: Ferment + 30 minutes   **Resting:** 1³/₄ hours   **2nd rising:** 45–60 minutes   **Baking:** 10–12 minutes
Freezing: Freezes well fully baked. Defrost at room temperature.

I was taking a bread class one day, when a guy called Mark Walpole knocked on the door and said: "I bought your book in the cheese shop down the road, and thought I would show you what I do." He gave me a bag of deep, wine-colored flour, which he told me he makes by drying and powdering the skins left over from wine-making in Canada, at a company he formed called Vinifera for Life. Apparently the flour is rich in anti-oxidants and fiber.

The next day I was making some bread for a gala dinner at The Priory hotel in Bath, and I thought it would be fun to experiment with the flour. I made some little baguettes using a mix of white flour, a little bit of rye flour, and some of the Cabernet grape flour, and the results were fantastic. It isn't just that the flour gives the bread a deep red/eggplant color, but it also gives a quite "meaty" tannic edge to the flavor, which works very well with charcuterie, hams, pâté, foie gras, cheese, and so on.

Makes 10 long rolls
You will need
350g (12oz.) white bread flour (about 2²/₃ cups)
180g (6oz.) red Cabernet grape flour (see page 17, 156)—about 1¹/₃ cups
50g (1³/₄oz.) dark rye flour (about 6 level tbsp.)
5g fresh yeast (about 1 level tsp.)
300g water (about 1¹/₂ cups)
50g full-bodied red wine, such as Cabernet Sauvignon (about ¹/₄ cup)
200g (7oz.) ferment (see Stages 1–4, pages 48–50) or fermented white dough (see page 73)
10g (¹/₃oz.) salt (about 2 level tsp.)
a little white flour for dusting, plus a little fine semolina, for dusting the peels

To prepare

Preheat the oven to 250°C/500°F. Unless you are going to bake in batches, you will need to use both shelves of the oven and put in 2 baking stones or baking trays, or one of each, to get good and hot.

Also, unless you are baking in batches, you will need enough peels or trays to load all the rolls before putting them into the oven.

Line 1 or 2 baking trays with couches or baking cloths.

To make

● Mix the flours together in a large mixing bowl and rub in the yeast with your fingertips (1). Add the water, wine, and ferment, then the salt, and mix well (2).

● When everything starts to come together into a dough, use your scraper to help you turn it out onto your work surface (don't flour the work surface first).

● Work the dough as on pages 24–6 (3), then flour your work surface lightly, place the dough on top, and form into a ball (see page 27) (4–5). Put the dough back into your (lightly floured) bowl, cover with a baking cloth, and let it rest for 1 hour.

● Lightly flour your work surface again, and then turn out the dough with the help of your scraper. Reshape it into a ball, and put it back into your (lightly floured) mixing bowl. Cover again with a baking cloth and let it rest for another 45 minutes (6).

● Divide the dough into 10 x 100g (3½oz.) pieces (see page 31).

● Shape the first piece into a small loaf shape (see page 32) (7) and place on a (lightly floured) couche or cloth-lined tray, seam-side down. Make a pleat in the couche or cloth, then shape the next roll and lay it on the tray, so that the pleat keeps it separate from the first one. Continue to form your rolls and pleat the couche/cloth so that none of the rolls touch each other (8).

● Cover with a baking cloth and let them rise for 45–60 minutes.

● Meanwhile, sprinkle some fine semolina onto your peels or trays.

● Place your rolls on the peels and make one long slash down the length of each (9).

● Open the oven door and quickly mist the inside of the oven with your water spray. Use your peels to slide your rolls onto the hot baking stones or trays in the oven, and spray some more before quickly closing the oven door. Turn the heat down to 230°C/450°F. Bake for 10–12 minutes until the crusts are well formed. The bread will look very dark, so don't panic and think it is ready before it really is. Take out the rolls and cool on a wire rack or in a wicker basket.

KHORASON FLOUR BREAD

I used to see bread made with khorason flour at local markets in France, and I've always liked its flavor—though it can be difficult to get hold of. When you combine khorason flour with white flour it gives a clean, fresh, wheaty taste to bread, and a slightly caramelly-toffee-ish flavor to the crust. I like it with soft cheese and salad.

Preparation: Ferment + 50 minutes   **Resting:** 130 minutes   **2nd rising:** 1 hour   **Baking:** 20–23 minutes
Freezing: Freezes well fully baked. Defrost at room temperature.

This recipe uses the autolyse method that I introduced in the previous chapter (see page 68), in which the flour and water are mixed together and then left to rest for 30 minutes before combining them with the rest of the ingredients.

Makes 5 small loaves
You will need
600g (21oz.) khorason flour (see page 17)—about
   4$^1/_2$–4$^2/_3$ cups
400g (14oz.) white bread flour (about 3 cups)
750g water (about 3$^3/_4$ cups)
200g (7oz.) fermented white dough (see page 73)
10g ($^1/_3$oz.) fresh yeast (about 2 level tsp.)
20g ($^2/_3$oz.) salt (about 4 level tsp.)
a little white flour, for dusting, plus a little semolina
   flour, for dusting the peels

To prepare
Preheat the oven to 250°C/500°F. Unless you are going to bake in batches, you will need to use both shelves of the oven and put in 2 baking stones or baking trays, or one of each, to get good and hot.
Also, unless you are baking in batches, you will need enough peels or trays to load all the loaves before putting

them into the oven. Line 2 or 3 large baking trays with couches or baking cloths.

To make

● Combine the flours in a large mixing bowl, then add the water and mix well. Let it rest for 30 minutes.

● Add the fermented dough and yeast, and mix together with your scraper. When everything starts to come together into a dough, use your scraper to help you turn it out onto your work surface (don't flour it first).

● Work the dough (see pages 24–6) for 5–8 minutes until it starts to become smooth. Sprinkle the salt on it and work it for another 4–5 minutes. By now the dough shouldn't be sticky, and should feel elastic and alive.

● Very lightly flour your work surface, and then form the dough into a ball (see page 27). Put the dough back into your (lightly floured) mixing bowl, cover with a baking cloth, and let it rest for 1¹/₂ hours (see page 28).

● Lightly flour your surface again and, with the help of your scraper, turn out the dough. Divide it into 5 x 380g (13-oz.) pieces (see page 31). Fold each piece (see page 27) then cover with a baking cloth and let them rest on your work surface for 10 minutes.

● Shape each piece of dough into a round loaf, using the method for forming into a ball, and place on your couche or cloth-lined trays. Let them rise for about 1 hour, or until just under double in volume.

● Sprinkle some fine semolina onto your peels and then place your loaves on top, seam-side down. Make 3 large slashes, like stripes, in the top of each (see page 37).

● Open the oven door and quickly mist the inside of the oven with your water spray. Use the peels to slide the loaves onto the hot baking stones or trays in the oven, and spray some more before quickly closing the oven door.

● Set the timer for 5 minutes. After this time, turn down the oven to 220°C/425ºF and bake for a further 15–18 minutes, until golden brown and the bottom of each loaf sounds hollow when tapped. Take out and cool on wire racks or in wicker baskets.

CIABATTA

I gave a recipe for ciabatta in my first book, *Dough*, using normal white bread flour, but as this is one of my favorite breads, I also wanted to include a version here.

Preparation: Ferment + 30–45 minutes   **Resting:** $1^1/_2$ hours   **2nd Rising:** 45–60 minutes   **Baking:** 18–20 minutes
Freezing: Three-quarter bake for around 12–15 minutes, cool and freeze. Then bake from frozen in a preheated oven at 200°C/400°F for 8–10 minutes. Cool as usual before eating.

This recipe uses specialty ciabatta flour, or a blend of half Italian 00 flour and half white bread flour. The dough is rested for longer and, as a result, has a stronger, slightly more characterful crust. The ferment used for ciabatta is known as biga in Italy, and it helps to give the bread its typical light, open texture.

Makes 4 loaves

FOR THE FERMENT
You will need
350g (12oz.) ciabatta flour—or half Italian 00 and half white bread flour (about $2^2/_3$ cups)
180g water (about 1 cup minus $1^1/_2$ tbsp.)
2g (approximately $^1/_4$ teaspoon) fresh yeast

To prepare
Combine the ingredients in a mixing bowl until you have a rough dough. Cover loosely with a large split freezer bag secured with an elastic band, and let it rest in a warm draft-free place for 17–24 hours.

FOR THE CIABATTA
You will need
450g (16oz.) ciabatta flour (or half Italian 00 and half white bread flour)—about $3^1/_3$ cups
10g ($^1/_3$oz.) fresh yeast (about 2 teaspoons)
all of the ferment
360g water (about $1^3/_4$ cups)
50g olive oil (5 tablespoons)
15g ($^1/_2$oz.) salt (3 level tsp.)
a little olive oil, for greasing
white flour or cornmeal, for dusting, plus a little fine semolina, for dusting the peels

To prepare
Preheat the oven to 250°C/500°F. Unless you are going to bake in batches, you will need to use both shelves of the oven and put in 2 baking stones or baking trays, or one of each, to get good and hot. Also, unless you are baking in batches, you will need enough peels or trays to load all the loaves before putting them into the oven. Line 2 large baking trays with couches or baking cloths.

To make

● Put the flour in a mixing bowl and rub in the yeast. Scoop the ferment into the bowl, and then add the water, oil and finally the salt, mixing well until everything is combined. Use your scraper to help you turn the dough out onto your work surface (don't flour it first).

● Work the dough (see pages 24–6) until it is supple and elastic and comes away from the work surface easily.

● Instead of flouring your mixing bowl, lightly oil it with olive oil, place the dough inside and let it rest for 1¹/₂ hours, covered with a baking cloth, until it has risen and feels bubbly and light.

● Flour your work surface generously with white flour or cornmeal and, with the help of the rounded end of your scraper, turn the dough out in one piece. Flour the top. Press the dough lightly and gently all over, dimpling it slightly with your fingers into a rectangular shape.

● Cut the dough into 5 roughly equal strips, and fold each strip into 3 to strengthen the dough. To do this, simply take each strip, fold one side into the middle and press down, then fold over again to the other side, and press down lightly to seal the edge. Roll lightly so that the seam of each piece is underneath.

● Place the pieces of dough, seam-side up, onto your (well-floured) couche or cloth-lined trays. Cover with more baking cloths and let rise for 45–60 minutes.

● Meanwhile, dust your peels or baking trays with fine semolina.

● Pick up one ciabatta at a time, turn it over so that the seam is underneath and stretch it lengthways just a little as you lay it on the peel or tray. (This stretch is what gives the bread its characteristic "slipper" shape.)

● Open the oven door and quickly mist the inside of your oven with your water spray (see page 22). Use the peels to slide your loaves onto the hot baking stones or trays in the oven, and spray some more before quickly closing the oven door. Turn down the heat to 220°C/425°F and bake for 18–20 minutes. Cool on wire racks.

PAIN BRIE

By now you have probably gotten used to me saying that a soft dough makes a light bread—well, this traditional bread from Normandy is the exact opposite! ▷

Preparation: Ferment + 45 minutes **Resting:** 1¹/₂ hours **2nd Rising:** 1 hour **Baking:** 20 minutes

When I was an apprentice in France, a new head baker from Normandy arrived at our bakery, and he introduced this bread, which traditionally sailors used to take to sea with them. Even though it would dry out while they were away, it would still taste good for a long time. What is interesting about Pain Brie is that to make it you begin with a very hard, stiff dough then pummel it repeatedly with a rolling pin, knocking out the air, so that it has a very close texture, and yet the finished bread is still light, tasty, and has a characterful, flavorful crust which is easy to digest. The word brie probably refers to the old tool which would once have been used for the bashing of the dough.

Makes 3 small loaves

You will need

10g (¹/₃oz.) fresh yeast (about 2 level tsp.)
50g water (about ¹/₄ cup)
900g (2lb.) fermented white dough (see page 73)
250g (9oz.) white bread flour (about 1³/₄–2 cups)
50g (1³/₄oz.) salted butter—or about 6 tbsp.
    unsalted plus 2 level tsp. salt
a little fine semolina, for dusting the peels

To prepare

Preheat your oven to 250°C/500°F at least 2 hours before you want to bake, and put in 2 baking stones or trays. You will need a baking tray lined with a couche or baking cloth to rise the loaves, and 2 or 3 peels or trays for transferring them to the oven.

To make

● Dissolve the yeast in the water. Place all the ingredients in a mixing bowl and combine really well. The dough will be very, very stiff but don't be tempted to add any extra water.

● Because the dough is so stiff, you won't be able to use the usual method of working the dough. Instead, you will have to use the English-style method of kneading: fold the dough over onto itself and then press really hard with the heel of your hand, and keep doing this for 1–2 minutes.

● Now it is time to use the rolling pin. Fold your dough onto itself and bring the rolling pin down hard across the dough (mind your fingers), then press it down with all the weight of your body (1). Keep folding and bashing (2) and pressing until, after about 15 minutes, the dough is smooth, velvety, and light—by which time, you will have had a really good workout!

● Now you can form the dough into a ball (see page 27) (3). You don't need any flour, as this dough won't stick at all. Put it into a clean bowl (again, don't flour it), cover with a baking cloth, and let it rest for 1¹/₂ hours.

● Still without using any flour, turn the dough out onto your work surface. Divide into 3 x 400g (14oz.) pieces (see page 31). Shape into round loaves by forming into a ball (see page 27). Lay, seam-side down, on your couche or cloth-lined tray, cover with more baking cloths and let rise for about 1 hour.

• Dust your peels or trays with fine semolina. Lift your loaves onto the peels or trays, and slash each one once lengthways down the middle. Now make a slightly shorter slash on either side, followed by another even shorter one on each side.

• Open the oven door and quickly mist the inside of the oven with your water spray. Use the peels to slide your loaves onto the hot baking stones or trays in the oven, and spray some more before quickly closing the oven door.

• Set your timer for 5 minutes. After this time, turn down the heat to 220°C/425°F and bake for another 15 minutes, until the loaves are golden brown, and the bottoms sound hollow when tapped. Cool on wire racks.

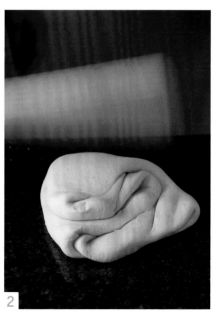

CHESTNUT FLOUR BREAD

Chestnut flour gives a great flavor to your bread, which you can really enhance by incorporating some whole cooked chestnuts. It also has a rich, dark brown color, which looks dramatic if you flour the tops of your loaves well, giving a lovely contrast of chocolate brown and white when the crusts burst. This bread looks very effective if you snip the top with a pair of scissors (page 37), or you can decorate it by cutting it with a blade or knife. This bread goes very well with strong, gamey casseroles, as well as strong cheese. I also like it toasted with scrambled eggs.

Preparation: Ferment + 45 minutes   **Resting:** 1¹/₂ hours   **2nd Rising:** 1¹/₂ hours   **Baking:** 25 minutes

For this recipe, I use the autolyse method (page 68) of mixing the flour and water first and then letting it rest for 30 minutes before adding the other ingredients.

Makes 4 small loaves

You will need

750g (26oz.) white bread flour (about 5¹/₂–
   5³/₄ cups)

400g (14oz.) chestnut flour (see page 18)—about
   3 cups

700g water (about 3¹/₂ cups)

450g (1lb.) fermented white dough (see page 73)

15g (¹/₂oz.) fresh yeast (about 3 level tsp.)

25g (1oz.) salt (about 2 level tbsp.)

200g (7oz.) whole, peeled vacuum-packed cooked
   chestnuts (about 1¹/₄ cups), crumbled into chunks

a little white flour, for dusting, plus a little fine
   semolina, for dusting the peels

a little butter or vegetable oil for pans

To prepare

Preheat the oven to 250°C/500°F. Unless you are going to bake in batches, you will need to use both shelves of the oven and put in 2 baking stones or baking trays, or one of each, to get good and hot. Also, unless you are baking in pans, you will need enough peels or trays to load all the loaves before putting them into the oven.

Depending on what style of loaves you want to make, either prepare 4 x 400g greased loaf pans, 4 bread-rising baskets or bowls lined with baking cloths, or 2 trays lined with couches or baking cloths (or go for a selection of all of them).

To make

● Combine the flours in a large bowl, add the water, and mix well for 5 minutes. Cover with a baking cloth and leave to rest for 30 minutes.

● Add the fermented dough and yeast and mix together, using your scraper. When everything begins to come together into a dough, use your scraper to help you turn it out onto your work surface (don't flour it first).

● Work the dough (see page 24–6) for 5–8 minutes until it starts to become smooth and elastic. Sprinkle the salt over it and work it for another 4–5 minutes. The dough shouldn't be sticky, and should feel elastic and alive.

● Very lightly flour your work surface. Place your dough on it, rough-side up, and flatten it out with your fingers. Spread the chestnut pieces over the top and press them down well into the dough. Fold a few times so that all the chestnuts are incorporated into the dough.

● Form the dough into a ball (see page 27), put back into your (lightly floured) mixing bowl, cover with a baking cloth, and let it rest for 40 minutes.

● Lightly flour your work surface again, and turn out the dough with the help of your scraper.

● Fold the dough (see page 28), then put back into your bowl, cover with your baking cloth, and let it rest for another 20 minutes.

● Lightly flour your work surface again, turn out the dough and divide into 4 x 630g (22oz.) pieces (see page 31). Shape into elongated loaves (see page 32), or round ones as if forming into a ball (see page 27). Roll the tops gently in some white flour and place on your couche or cloth-lined trays, or in greased pans, as you like. Don't worry the dough will fit into your pans. Alternatively, form into balls and put into well-floured bread-rising baskets or cloth-lined bowls. Let rise, covered with baking cloths, for 1$\frac{1}{2}$ hours or until just under double in volume.

● Sprinkle some fine semolina onto your peels or trays and then place any loaves that aren't in pans on top. Either snip the tops with sharp scissors or slash with a lame or sharp knife (see page 37)—you don't need to slash the tops of loaves in pans.

● Open the oven door and quickly mist the inside of the oven with your water spray. Put in your pans, and/or slide the loaves onto the hot baking stones or trays in the oven, and spray some more before quickly closing the oven door.

● Set your timer for 5 minutes. After this time, turn down the temperature to 220°C/440°F and bake for another 20 minutes. The bread is ready when it is the color of deep brown leather and the bottom of each loaf sounds hollow when tapped underneath. Cool on wire racks or wicker baskets,

BAGELS

Bagels seem to be particularly fashionable at the moment, and homemade ones make a great snack with whatever filling you prefer, from cream cheese to smoked salmon (lox). ▷

Preparation: Ferment + 30 minutes   **Resting:** 20 minutes   **2nd Rising:** 30–60 minutes
Baking: 10–13 minutes

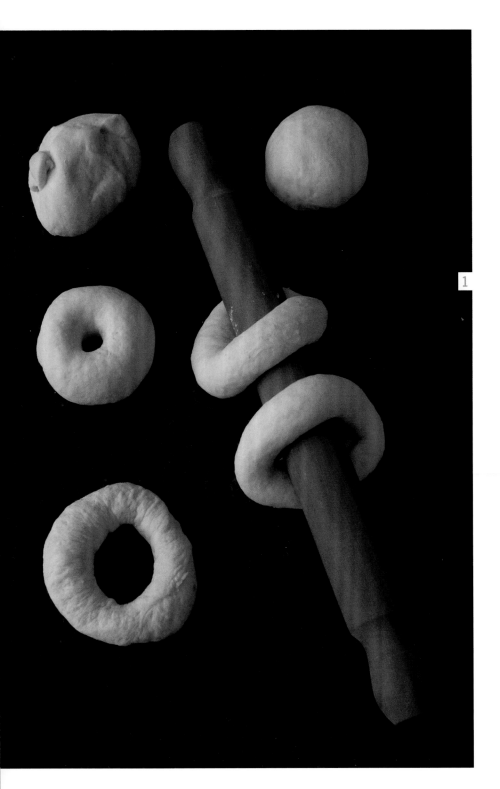

The dough is boiled before baking to give it that characteristic chewy bite and shine. The baking soda is entirely optional, but it helps with the texture, color, and sheen.

Makes 12

You will need

either 300g (11oz.) fermented white dough (see page 73) or 200g (7oz.) white bread flour (about 1 cup), 5g fresh yeast (1 level tsp.), and 100g water (about 1/2 cup), mixed together and left to ferment for at least 2 hours at room temperature

550g (19oz.) white bread flour (about 4–41/4 cups)

10g (1/3oz.) salt (about 2 level tsp.)

20g (2/3oz.) good honey (1 tsp.)

250g water (about 11/4 cups)

a little white flour, for dusting

a little baking soda (optional)

poppy seeds and/or sesame seeds, for the topping (optional)

a little vegetable oil

To prepare

Preheat the oven to 240°C/425°F.

You will need a rolling pin and 2 baking trays lined with parchment paper lightly oiled with vegetable oil.

Tip the poppy seeds and/or sesame seeds (if using) into separate bowls, wide enough for you to press the tops of the bagels into them.

To make

● Mix together the dough, flour, salt, honey, and water in a mixing bowl with your scraper. When everything starts to come together into a dough (it will be quite stiff), use your scraper to help you turn it out onto your work surface (don't flour it first).

● Work the dough (see pages 24–6) until it is smooth and elastic.

● Lightly flour your work surface, and then form the dough into a ball (see page 27). Put the dough back into your (lightly floured) mixing bowl, cover with a baking cloth and let it rest for 20 minutes.

● Lightly flour your surface again, turn out the dough, and divide it into around 12 x 80g (3oz.) pieces (see page 31).

● To shape the pieces into bagels, first form each piece into a small ball (see page 27). Make a hole in the center of each ball by forcing the end of your rolling pin through the dough (1) and rolling it around a little to smooth the edges around the hole.

● Lay the bagels on your lightly oiled parchment-lined trays (2). Cover with a large split plastic freezer bag or a baking cloth and let rise for 30–60 minutes.

● Bring a large pot of water to a boil. Add 1 teaspoon baking soda (if using) to every quart of water.

● Plunge the bagels into the boiling water for 30 seconds, then turn them over using tongs or a spoon and leave for another 30 seconds on the other side (3). Drain, dip one side only into sesame seeds or poppy seeds (4), and then lay them, seed-side up, back on the baking trays (5).

● Put the trays into the oven and bake for about 10 minutes if you like them quite chewy inside; leave them in 3 minutes longer if you want them more crunchy. You may need to turn the trays around in the oven halfway through baking time, so the bagels brown evenly all over. Cool on a wire rack.

PRETZELS

Everybody seems to love pretzels, which originally hailed from the region around southern Germany and Alsace somewhere in the 11th–13th centuries. All sorts of stories are told about their origins. Some say they were first made by monks and their shape represents arms folded across the chest in prayer (they were supposed to have been given to good children as rewards), but as with all these old recipes, who really knows?

Preparation: Ferment + 20–30 minutes **Resting:** 1 hour **2nd Rising:** 45–60 minutes
Baking: 10–12 minutes **Freezing:** Freeze well fully baked. Defrost at room temperature.

Makes 12

You will need
400g (14oz.) fermented white dough (see
  page 73)
500g (18oz.) white bread flour (about 3³/₄ cups)
10g (¹/₃oz.) fresh yeast (about 2 level tsp.)
15g (¹/₂oz.) sugar (about 3³/₄ tsp.)
10g (¹/₃oz.) salt (about 2 level tsp.)
50g (1³/₄oz.) unsalted butter (about 3¹/₂ tsp.)
100g milk (about ¹/₂ cup)
100g water (about ¹/₂ cup)
1 egg mixed with a pinch of salt (and, if you like, a
  few drops of coffee essence for color) 1 hour
  before you need it, to make an egg wash
a little vegetable oil
a little coarse salt such as kosher, for sprinkling

To prepare
Preheat the oven to 250°C/500°F.
  Lightly oil 1 or 2 large baking trays.

To make
● Mix all the ingredients together in your mixing bowl.

The resulting dough will feel very stiff. Cover the bowl with a baking cloth and let it rest for 1 hour.

● Very lightly flour your work surface. Divide the dough (see page 31) into 12 x 100g (3¹/₂oz.) pieces.

● Roll each piece with your fingers until it is around 20cm (8in.) long. Form into a heart shape by bringing the 2 ends to the center, crossing the right end over the left, bringing it back underneath, then laying the ends either side of the point of the heart.

● Lay the pretzels on a greased baking tray and glaze with egg wash. Let rise, uncovered, for 45–60 minutes.

● Glaze again with egg wash and sprinkle immediately with coarse salt, pressing it down into the dough a little.

● Put the pretzels into the oven and turn down the heat to 230°C/450°F. Bake for 10–12 minutes, until they are dark golden brown, at which point they will be chewy. If you prefer them a little crispier, give them another couple of minutes. Cool on a wire rack.

BUCKWHEAT BLINIS

Although blinis contain yeast, the mixture is more of a batter than a dough. Serve them with smoked salmon, some sprigs of fresh dill and, if you like, a little spoonful of fish roe eggs, which look like caviar.

Preparation: 30 minutes **Resting:** $3^1/2$ hours **Cooking:** 1–2 minutes

You can use blini pans, if you have them, or dot spoonfuls of the batter around a large frying pan. If I am serving blinis as canapés, I make them roughly 3cm ($1^1/4$in.) in diameter; as an appetizer, I make them about 10cm (4in.) in diameter.

Makes 10–12 small ones or 6 large ones

You will need
75g ($2^2/3$oz.) buckwheat flour
   (about $1/2$ cup)
75g ($2^2/3$oz.) white bread flour
5g salt (about 1 level tsp.)
150g milk (about $3/4$ cup)
7g ($1/4$oz.) fresh yeast
2 large eggs
80g crème fraîche (about $1/3$ cup)
vegetable oil (and half a potato),
   for greasing

To prepare
Oil your blini pans. I use a trick I learned growing up in Brittany, watching my grandmother oil pans for crêpes, which is to dip a cut potato into cooking oil and, holding it with a fork, rub over the surface of the pan. It gives you just the right thin film of oil (see pic).

To make
● Combine the flours and the salt in a mixing bowl.

● Pour the milk into a pan and place it on the stove to heat. Bring it to just boiling point and then remove from the heat. Crumble the yeast into the milk.

● Separate the eggs and set the whites aside. Add the yolks to the milk in the pan, along with the sour cream. Pour this mixture slowly into the flour, stirring well as you do so, until you have a thick batter.

● Cover the bowl with a baking cloth and let it rest for $1^1/2$ hours until the batter has risen and looks bubbly and spongy.

● Beat the egg whites to soft peaks and let it fold gently into the batter. Cover the bowl again and let it rest for another 2 hours.

● To cook, get your oiled pans hot and pour in a small puddle of batter, if using blini pans, or several puddles if using a large pan. (You should be able to fit 4–6 canapé-sized blinis, or 2 larger ones, in the pan at the same time.) When the batter starts to form bubbles (about 30 seconds for small ones, 1 minute for large), turn the blinis over and cook for the same amount of time until light golden brown on the other side. Remove from the pan and cool on a wire rack.

JAPANESE "SUSHI" ROLLS

These are fun little rolls, fantastic served with a glass of chilled sake before a meal, to hand around at a party, or with some marinated seared salmon with a little wasabi and pickled ginger as an appetizer.

Preparation: 40 minutes   **Resting:** 1 hour   **2nd Rising:** 30–45 minutes   **Baking:** 10–15 minutes
Freezing: Not recommended.

I am quite intrigued by sake—not the kind that is served hot in Chinese restaurants and noodle bars, but the very sophisticated, premium and vintage sake that in Japan is considered the equivalent to serious wine. Fortunately, it is now being brought over to Britain in limited quantities thanks to two French sommeliers, Xavier Chapelou and Jean-Louis Naveilhan, and a Japanese sake expert Kumiko Ohta, who together have formed a small company called Isaké (see page 156). They are importing some amazing examples never seen before outside Japan, and are making it their mission to show how these sakes, which are drunk chilled in wine glasses, can be matched with European, as well as Japanese food.

I did some experimenting with some of them and came up with this recipe for little nori seaweed bread rolls, inspired by sushi.

You will only need to use half the quantity of dough given in this recipe, but as it is very difficult to mix and work a smaller quantity, I suggest you keep the rest and use it to make a ferment (see page 47).

Makes 10–12 rolls

You will need

10g (¹/₃oz.) fresh yeast (about 2 level tsp.)

500g (18oz.) white bread flour (about 3³/₄ cups)

10g (¹/₃oz.) salt (about 2 level tsp.)

350g water (about 1³/₄ cups)

75g good-quality sake (¹/₃ cup)

1 x 11g package sushi nori (five 8 x 8in. sheets)

30–40g (1–1¹/₂oz.) sesame seeds (3¹/₂-4¹/₂ tbsp.)

a little finely-ground cornmeal, for dusting

a little vegetable oil

To prepare

You need a rolling pin, and a couple of lightly oiled baking trays. Preheat the oven to 250°C/500°F.

To make

● Rub the yeast into the flour with your fingertips, add the salt and the water, and mix well using your scraper until everything starts to come together into a dough. Use your scraper to help you turn it out onto your work surface (don't flour it first).

● Work the dough (see pages 24–6), form it into a ball (see page 27), put it back into your (lightly floured) bowl, cover with a baking cloth, and let it rest for 1 hour.

● Lightly flour your work surface with cornmeal, and turn out the dough with the help of your scraper. Roll out the dough using a rolling pin to around 5mm (¹/₄in.) thick, sprinkle with a little sake, then cover with sheets of seaweed (tearing them to fit if necessary) so that all the dough is covered. Sprinkle again with enough sake to soak the seaweed well, and then scatter the sesame seeds liberally over the top.

● Roll up the seaweed-covered dough like a jelly roll, then cut into slices about 1cm (¹/₂ inch) thick, using a sharp knife with a serrated blade. Lay the slices, leaving plenty of room in between, on your baking trays, cover with a dishtowel and let rise for around 30–45 minutes.

● Open the oven door and quickly mist the inside of the oven with your water spray. Put in your trays of rolls, spray some more before quickly closing the oven door. Bake for 10–15 minutes until light golden, then transfer onto wire racks or wicker baskets to cool completely.

FLAMICHE

In some parts of eastern France, especially Champagne and Lorraine, they say that they were making this kind of flatbread with a savory topping long before the Italians made pizza famous. Nowadays there is a vogue for "pizza blanche," which is made with pizza dough, but still with this "white" crème fraîche based topping rather than a tomato based one. If you like, you can simply mix some cooked spinach into the eggs and crème fraîche, instead of pancetta or lardons.

Preparation: 45 minutes   **Resting:** 1 hour   **Baking:** 15–20 minutes

Makes 1 large flamiche—enough for a snack for 12, or a light lunch

FOR THE DOUGH
You will need
10g (¹/₃oz.) fresh yeast (about 2 level tsp.)
500g (18oz.) white bread flour (about 3³/₄ cups)
10g (¹/₃oz.) salt (about 2 level tsp.)
350g water (about 1³/₄ cups)
a little white flour, for dusting

FOR THE TOPPING
You will need
1 tablespoon olive oil
200g (7oz.) sliced bacon or pancetta
2 leeks, finely sliced
3 eggs
300g (11oz.) crème fraîche (about 1¹/₂ cups)
salt, pepper, and nutmeg, to taste
a little grated Gruyère (optional)

To prepare
Preheat the oven to 230°C/450°F. You will need a large, lipped baking tray.

To make
• Rub the yeast into the flour using your fingertips, add the salt and the water and mix well, using your scraper, until everything starts to come together. Use your scraper to help you turn out the dough onto your work surface (don't flour it first).

• Work the dough (see pages 24–6), then form into a ball (see page 27) and put back into your (lightly floured) bowl. Cover with a baking cloth and let it rest for 1 hour.

• Lightly flour your baking tray and turn your dough out onto it with the help of your scraper. Using your fingertips, flatten and dimple the dough to fit the tray. Ridge the edges all the way round, so that they are quite high and will contain the topping you are going to add.

• To make the topping, heat the olive oil in a frying pan, put in the bacon or pancetta and sauté until it starts to color. Remove from the pan, and then put in the leeks, sautéing them gently until they start to color a little. Mix the eggs and crème fraîche together in a bowl, add the cooked bacon and leeks, and season to taste with salt, pepper, and nutmeg. Spread the mixture all over the dough. If you like, you can scatter some grated Gruyère over the top as well.

• Put the flamiche into the oven and bake for 15–20 minutes until golden brown with crispy edges. (Check it after 10 minutes to make sure it is browning evenly and move it around in the oven as necessary.)

• Take the flamiche out of the oven and transfer to a wire rack to cool slightly. Cut into slices and eat while still warm.

4

SWEET

In France, most of the recipes in this chapter would be united under the rather grand title of Viennoiserie, which is used to describe the kind of treats that are made with a sweet dough containing yeast, and is distinct from Pâtisserie, which includes desserts as well as anything made with pastry. However, I've included a couple of favorites which don't contain yeast—Far Breton, from my native Brittany, and some fantastic ginger biscuits, brilliant for hanging on the tree at Christmas.

CROISSANTS

The story I grew up with about the origin of croissants is that they were made to commemorate the defeat of the Turkish army by the Austrians at the siege of Vienna.

The story goes that during the night, a baker heard some rumbling noises and raised the alarm. The sounds turned out to be Turkish soldiers digging tunnels under the walls of the city. To celebrate the foiling of the plot, the King told the baker to create a sweet dough in the shape of a crescent, the emblem on the Turkish flag. The Viennese took the idea with them to Paris and from there the French made croissants their own.

In France, broadly speaking, we have two different styles of croissant. The ones you might find in a patisserie tend to be quite refined, very layered, light, and open textured. The croissant you find in a typical bakery tends to be a bit more doughy and rustic. When I was an apprentice, like most bakers, we would make two versions—the "straighter" one, made with pure butter, and the less expensive, exaggeratedly curved one, known as "ordinaire," which would be made with margarine.

What is the perfect croissant? After all, you find so many variations, even throughout France. I would say, crisp and flaky on the outside, with well-defined layers, and a soft, airy, buttery inside.

Like sourdough, there is something about making croissants that really seems to capture the imagination. People see it as a kind of quest that may not produce fantastic results the first time, but after a bit of practice will give them something to be really proud of.

Ideally you need 2 days, or 1 very long day, to make croissants, because the dough must be rested before you start rolling it and then folding it around your butter. The thing that most people struggle with is rolling the dough without it sticking, and the key here is to allow time for the dough and butter to get to the same (chilled)

temperature before you put them together. That way, the dough stays firm and easy to work with.

The quality of the butter is important because its flavor will characterize the croissant—you want something refined, creamy, and nutty, rather than something that will give a fatty, greasy taste. I use French unsalted butter from the Charente or Normandy, which has a lovely creaminess to it. Unsalted butter is harder than salted and so helps to keep the dough firm. Soft butter, on the other hand, will melt and make the croissants greasy, especially if you are making them in warm weather. If you put your thumb on top of a pack of butter straight from the fridge, a fattier, greasy butter will make a dent immediately. One of the reasons that many bakeries began to use margarine in their croissants is that the firmer and more elastic the fat is, the easier it is to work the dough—but, of course, the flavor of margarine is inferior, and some brands still contain trans-fats, which we now know to be bad for us.

I wouldn't try working with less—or any more—than 1kg (2¹/₂lb.) dough because it will be too difficult to roll. The dough needs to be worked as little as possible, because you want to keep the lamination—that is, the layers of dough, butter, dough, butter. And you need a good space, such as a long table or work surface.

You can freeze croissants either once they are shaped and before they have risen (you will need to de-frost them before rising) or after they have risen, in which case, glaze them after rising and bake from frozen at 220°C/425°F for 18–20 minutes the next morning. Alternatively bake them fully, freeze them, and defrost as above, then just pop them into the oven at 200°C/400°F for a few minutes to crisp up.

Preparation: Approximately 1 hour   **Resting:** 3–13½ hours   **2nd Rising:** 2 hours   **Baking:** 18–20 minutes
Freezing: See page 116

Makes 12–14 croissants

You will need

20g (⅔oz.) fresh yeast (about 4 level tsp.)

500g (18oz.) white bread flour (about 3¾ cups)

10g (⅓oz.) salt (about 2 level tsp.)

50g (1¾oz.) sugar (¼ cup)

55g (2oz.) egg (shelled weight), equivalent to
   1 large egg

125g cold whole milk (about ⅔ cup)

125g water (about ⅔ cup)

200g (7oz) good-quality, unsalted butter, straight
   from the fridge—¾ cup plus 2 tbsp. (use the
   wrapper for greasing the trays)

1 egg mixed with a pinch of salt an hour before
   you need it, to make an egg wash

To prepare

You need a plastic tray or cutting board that will fit in the fridge, and two baking trays, lightly greased with butter.

To make

● Put the flour into a mixing bowl and rub in the yeast with your fingertips, then stir in the salt and sugar. Add the egg, milk, and water and mix together, using your scraper. When everything starts to come together into a dough, use your scraper to help you turn it out onto your work surface (don't flour it first).

● Work the dough (see pages 24–6) for 3–4 minutes.

● Form the dough into a ball (see page 27) and cut a cross in the top with a knife (1). Put back into your (lightly floured) mixing bowl. Cover with a large, split freezer bag secured with an elastic band, and let it rest in the fridge for at least 2 hours, but preferably overnight (12 hours).

● Lightly flour your work surface, take the dough out of the mixing bowl and, starting at the center where you have made your cross, roll out the 4 corners of the dough (2–3).

● Open the butter, but leave it sitting on its wrapper, and place a split freezer bag over the top. Flatten the butter into a square shape with a rolling pin by tapping it gently (the bag will protect your rolling pin from becoming greasy). Turn the butter over, wrapper and all, and tap again. until around 1cm (½in.) thick. It should be big enough to fill the center area of your rolled dough.

● Lift off the wrapper and use the freezer bag to lift up the flattened butter and turn it over into the center of the rolled out dough (4)—the aim here is to touch the butter as little as possible to avoid warming it up. Lift off the bag. One at a time, fold in the 4 sides of the dough over the top of the flattened butter (5–6).

● Using your rolling pin, and rolling lengthways only, roll out the dough (7) into a rectangle making it 2–3 times longer than its original length (about 60–70cm—23½–27½in.). Keep your hands at either end of the rolling pin, outside the area of the dough, and be very gentle—this helps to distribute the pressure more evenly, so the dough ends up the same thickness all over. (If you place your fingers in the center of the pin, the pressure will make a dent in the center of the dough.) Each time you roll, lift the dough a little and move it around slightly on your work surface, to dry it out underneath and help prevent it from sticking.

● Fold the dough into thirds (8). I make an indent in the top of the dough (9) to remind myself that I am at the first folding stage. Place on your plastic tray or board, cover with a large split freezer bag and let it rest for 20–30 minutes in the fridge.

● Take the dough out of the fridge and set it on your lightly floured work surface with the short end facing you. Use your rolling pin to roll it lengthways only as before (10), then fold into thirds again (I now make 2 indents in the top) and let it rest for another 20–30 minutes in the fridge.

● Repeat the rolling and resting process one more time (making 3 indents in the top of the dough), and then roll out your dough into a rectangle 30 x 75cm (12 x 30in.), and 4mm (1/5in.) thick. With a large knife, cut the dough lengthways down the center and trim the edges (11).

● Now you need to cut each strip into 6–7 triangles, making the base of each triangle about 9cm (3½in.) and the sides roughly 15cm (6in.) (12).

● Make a tiny vertical cut in the base of each triangle (13). This little split will help you to form the croissant shape, as you roll up your dough.

● Start to roll up each triangle from the bottom, pulling very gently at the split you have made (14–15). Don't crush the dough, if you have rolled it properly, you should be able to unroll it just as easily. Continue rolling briefly by sliding your fingers over the top, gently (16).

● Preheat your oven to 220–230°C/425–450°F.

● Glaze the tops of the croissants with egg wash, brushing lightly from the center outwards towards the tips—this is so that you don't get an excess of egg sticking the folds together. Place the croissants on your greased trays, leaving ample space between them to allow for expansion while they are rising (17).

● Let the croissants rise in a warm place such as a cupboard, a big drawer, or a turned off microwave for about 2 hours. (An enclosed place well out of drafts is best, as you don't want a crust to form on top, and if you cover the croissants with a baking cloth it will stick to the egg glaze. If you don't have anywhere suitable, then don't glaze the croissants at this stage, cover them with a baking cloth during proving, and glaze twice before baking.) Don't rush the rising process, because if the dough becomes too warm it will start to ooze butter, making the croissants heavy and fatty, rather than flaky.

● Glaze again with egg wash (18) and bake for 18–20 minutes until golden. Cool on wire racks.

VARIATIONS

Pain au chocolat, pain aux raisins, and abricotine are all made using croissant dough—only the finishing is different—and they all come under the generic heading of viennoiserie.

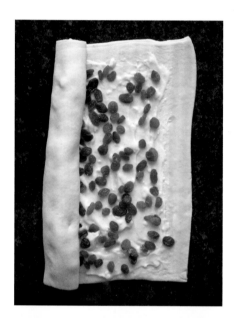

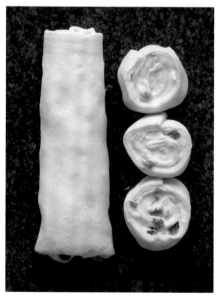

I suggest that whenever you make a batch of croissant dough, you make some plain croissants and some of the variations, depending on your mood and the ingredients you have on hand. They use varying amounts of crème pâtissière and, in the case of the pears, crème d'amande. Any left over crème pâtissière can be used as a dip for Snippets (page 128) or in Le Pudding (page 154).

Pain aux raisins

To make around 15 you will need half the quantity of croissant dough and around 350g (12oz.—half a batch) crème pâtissière on page 143, about 1 cup golden raisins, and some sugar syrup, see page 143.

Follow the croissant recipe, up to the final rolling out, then roll the dough into a rectangle of about 30 x 40cm (12 x 16in.). Set it in front of you, with the long edge toward you.

Spread each rectangle all over with crème pâtissière, leaving a clean strip along the long edge closest to you. Sprinkle the raisins over the crème pâtissière.

Starting from the long edge furthest from you, roll up the dough towards you like a jelly roll. Brush the clean edge closest to you with egg wash and fold it up and over, pressing down a little to seal. Turn the filled roll over so that the seam is underneath and cut into around 15 slices 1½–2cm (about ¾in.) thick, using a sharp metal scraper or pastry knife. Lay the slices on greased baking trays cut-side up, cover with a baking cloth, and let rise for 1½ hours. Glaze as for croissants, pressing each pain aux raisins down a little with your pastry brush. Bake as for croissants. Take out and glaze with sugar syrup while still warm. Cool on wire racks.

Abricotines

To make around 9, you will need half the quantity of croissant dough and around 150g (5oz.—quarter of a batch) crème pâtissière on page 143, and either 9 fresh apricot halves (in season) poached until soft in a little sugar syrup (see page 143), or canned apricots (out of season). Your oven temperature should be slightly lower (210°C/400°F).

Follow the recipe for croissants, up to the final rolling out, then roll the dough into a square of 30 x 30cm (12 x 12in.). Cut into 10cm (4in.) squares (1).

Set a square of dough out in front of you, and fold 1 corner into the center (2) and then the opposite. Put a good teaspoon of crème pâtissière in the middle over the point where the 2 corners meet, and then place half a poached apricot on top (3). Put the abricotines on greased baking trays, cover with a baking cloth and let rise for 1–1½ hours. Brush with egg wash and bake at 210°C/400°F for 15–16 minutes.

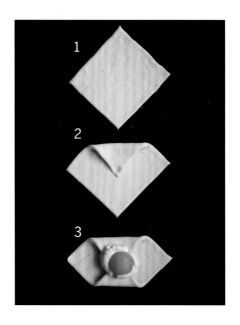

Variation, with pear

For these variations, I like to make a slightly more complicated shape, although you can stick with the abricotine shape, if you prefer. As well as substituting poached fresh pears, or canned ones (out of season), I also use a mixture of around 175g (6oz.—a quarter of the recipe) crème pâtissière and 125g (4 ½oz.—a quarter of the recipe) crème d'amande (page 143).

I will try to explain the folding technique in words, but the pictures should make it clearer! Start with a 10cm (4in.) square, as before (1), then fold this into a triangle (2). Turn the triangle so that the tip is facing you and then cut along the 2 shorter sides, leaving a border of around 5mm (¼in.) and stopping just short of the tip (3), so that the cuts don't actually meet, and the border is still attached. Unfold the triangle, and you should have a diamond within a diamond, still attached at the top and bottom (4). Fold the left-hand border over the inner diamond (5), then fold the right-hand border over the top of that. By doing this, you create little twisted handles at the top and bottom of the diamond shape. Put some of the crème pâtissière and crème d'amande mixture in the center, top with a pear (6), then let rise and bake as for abricotines.

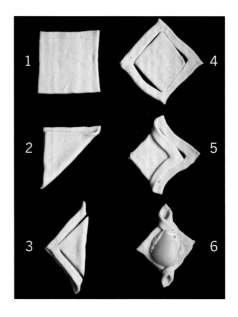

Pain au chocolat

To make about 14, you will need around 1½ x 150g (5oz.) bars of good-quality chocolate (70% cocoa solids) so that you can get 14 strips of chocolate. I use bars that break into strips of 3 x 5g (¼oz.) squares, which is perfect. Follow the recipe for croissants up to the point of cutting your rolled rectangle of dough (around 30 x 75cm —12 x 30in.) lengthways into two strips. Instead of cutting your strips of dough into triangles, cut each strip crossways into 7 rectangles about 10cm (4in.) wide (so you end up with 14 rectangles approximately 15 x 10cm—6 x 4in.). Lay out the rectangles, long side facing you.

Break your chocolate bars into strips of around 3 squares (just shorter than your dough) and place a strip on each rectangle, about 2cm (1¾in.) from the left-hand edge (1). Fold the edge of the dough over the top of the chocolate (2) and then fold over again, pressing the edges together to seal (3). Lay seam-side down on greased baking trays to rise, as for croissants, and glaze and bake in the same way.

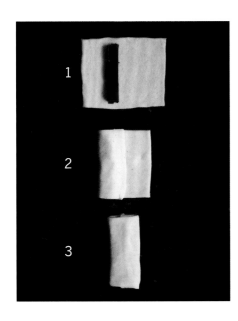

ALMOND CROISSANTS

The best way to make these is with croissants you have bought (good-quality) or made that have been left to dry out for 2–3 days. Fresh ones will be too soft and will simply collapse under the filling and topping.

Freezing: You can make these up and freeze before or after baking. Either way defrost overnight on a tray in a cold oven, then either bake at 190°C/375°F for 8–10 minutes or, if fully baked, pop into the oven for a few minutes to crisp up.

You will also need some sugar syrup (see page 143), some crème d'amande (page 143) and some slivered almonds.

Cut your croissants in half lengthways, and then put the 2 halves, cut-side up, on your work surface. Brush the cut sides with sugar syrup, so that it soaks well into the pastry. Spread the inside of one half with crème d'amande (a couple of tablespoons should be enough), and then sandwich the 2 halves back together again. Holding the reassembled croissant in one hand, use a butter knife to spread another couple of tablespoons of crème d'amande over the top, and sprinkle with slivered almonds.

Bake in a preheated oven at 190°C/375°F for around 8–10 minutes, until the almonds on top have turned nicely golden.

(If you want something really rich, you can do the same thing with sliced pains au chocolat. Again, they need to be 2–3 days old.)

Snippets

Kids love these (pictured left). Simply cut any trimmings of dough from making croissants, etc. into strips about 2cm (1in.) wide, and then twist them a few times. Heat some vegetable oil in a pan (no more than a third full), and quickly deep-fry the strips until they are golden brown. Drain them well on paper towels and roll in sugar and cinnamon while still hot. Cool slightly, and serve with a little bowl of crème pâtissière (page 143) or jam, for dipping into.

Savory variations

To make ham and cheese, mushroom or spinach croissants, follow the instructions for almond croissants (page 126), but omit the sugar syrup and use béchamel sauce (see page 143) in place of the crème pâtissière. Spread the béchamel on each cut half of croissant, and top one half with a slice of good ham, some cooked spinach, or a spoonful of cooked mushrooms, then grate some Emmental cheese or Swiss cheese over it. Sandwich the 2 halves back together again, and use your butter knife to spread some more béchamel over the top, finishing with a little more grated Emmental. Bake in a pre-heated oven (like almond croissants) at 190°C/375°F for 8–10 minutes.

STOLLEN

This is a delicious bread, traditional at Christmas time. As it keeps well, you can make it up to a week in advance—beware, though, its pretty irresistible, so you might find it gets eaten before the festivities. **Freezing:** Freezes well fully baked. Defrost at room temperature. ▷

Preparation: 45 minutes   Resting: 1$1/2$–2 hours   2nd rising: 2–2$1/2$ hours   Baking: 30–35 minutes

Makes 3 stollen

You will need
1kg (2$1/4$lb.) white bread flour (about 7$1/2$ cups)
20g ($2/3$oz.) fresh yeast (about 4 level tsp.)
500g milk, at body temperature (about 2$1/2$ cups)
200g (7oz.) unsalted butter (1 cup minus 2 tbsp.)—
     use the wrapper for greasing
50g (1$3/4$oz.) sugar ($1/4$ cup)
10g ($1/3$oz.) salt (about 2 level tsp.)
220g (8oz.) egg (shelled weight), roughly
     equivalent to 4 large eggs
1 batch of crème d'amande (see page 143)
400g (14oz.) natural (uncolored) marzipan (about
     1$1/4$ cups), cut into small pieces

FOR THE FILLING
180g (6oz.) golden raisins (about 1$1/3$ cups)
100g (3$1/2$oz.) glacé cherries (about $3/4$ cup)
200g (7oz.) candied peel (about 1$1/2$ cups)
60g (2oz.) toasted slivered almonds ($1/2$ cup)
4 tablespoons rum
1 teaspoon cinnamon

FOR THE GLAZE
100g (3$1/2$oz.) butter ($1/2$ cup minus 1 tbsp.)
2 capfuls rum
confectioners' sugar, for dusting

To prepare
Preheat the oven to 170°C/350°F. You will need a large baking tray, greased with butter.

To make
● Place the flour in a mixing bowl and crumble in the yeast with your fingers. Mix in the milk, butter, sugar, salt, and eggs, using your scraper to combine everything together. When the mixture starts to come together into a dough, use your scraper to turn it out onto your work surface (don't flour it first). Work the dough (see page 24–6).

● Lightly flour your work surface, and then form the dough into a ball (see page 27). Put it back into your (lightly floured) mixing bowl, cover with a baking cloth. and let it rest for 1–1$1/2$ hours.

● Again, lightly flour your work surface. Turn out the dough with the help of your scraper and use your fingertips to flatten it into a rough square shape.

● In another bowl, mix together all the ingredients for the filling. Spread your filling over the dough, and fold a few times to incorporate fully. Form the dough into a ball, and put back into your (lightly floured) mixing bowl to rest for another 30 minutes.

● Again, lightly flour the work surface and turn out the dough. Cut into 3 equal pieces.

● Put each piece of dough, smooth-side down, onto your lightly floured surface and flatten out with your fingertips into a rectangle roughly 20 x 15cm (8 x 6in.). Spread the top of each piece of dough generously with crème d'amande, and then scatter with pieces of marzipan.

● Working with each stollen at a time, fold one of the long sides into the center (over the cream and marzipan filling), then fold the other side over the top and press down all around the edges to seal. Place the filled stollens, seam-side down, on your greased baking tray. Cover with a baking cloth and let rise for 2–2$1/2$ hours until just under double in volume.

● Put the tray of stollen into the oven and bake for 30–35 minutes until light golden. Just before they come out of the oven, make up the glaze. Melt the butter in a small pan and stir in the rum. Take the stollen out of the oven and brush quite heavily with the glaze while still hot. Immediately dust thickly with icing sugar. Cool on a wire rack.

BRIOCHE

Brioche has become very fashionable in the U.K., whereas in northern France it is still considered as a Sunday treat, rather than an everyday bread. Each bakery has its own special recipe, which will taste subtly different thanks to the particular flavor of the local butter, or the baker's technique. Sometimes you will see round buns, sometimes they will be shaped to resemble little balls with even smaller balls, like little heads, on top—we call these brioche à tête. Alternatively, you can bake several buns together in one loaf pan where they will grow and graft together to form one bobbly loaf (left).

Preparation: 45 minutes   **Resting:** 14–16 hours   **2nd rising:** 2¹/₂ hours   **Baking:** 10 minutes for buns and 35–40 minutes for a loaf   **Freezing:** Freezes well fully baked. Defrost at room temperature.

Makes around 15 buns, 2 loaves,
or 1 loaf and 10 buns

FOR THE DOUGH

You will need

500g (18oz.) white bread flour (about 3³/₄ cups)

50g (1³/₄oz.) sugar (¹/₄ cup)

15g (¹/₂oz.) fresh yeast (about 3 level tsp.)

10g (¹/₃oz.) salt (about 2 level tsp.)

350g (12 oz.) egg (shelled weight), roughly
    equivalent to 6 large eggs

250g (9oz.) unsalted cold butter (1 cup)—use the
    wrapper for greasing

1 egg beaten with a pinch of salt 1 hour
    before it is needed, to make an egg wash

To prepare

Cut the butter into small cubes and leave next to you ready to use. You will need some metal or, preferably, bendy silicone brioche trays—either 15 individual ones, or several trays holding 6 or 12 buns in each. If making loaves you will need one or two 400g (14oz.) loaf pans, lightly greased with butter. Metal pans will need greasing.

To make

- Put the flour, sugar, yeast, and salt into your mixing bowl, rub in the yeast, then add the eggs and combine really well with the help of your scraper (1). When everything starts to come together into a dough, use your scraper to help you turn it out onto your work surface (don't flour it first).

- Work the dough (see page 24–6). It will look and feel very messy and sticky to begin with, but after a while it will come alive and start to come away from your work surface and fingers easily. At this point scatter the butter over the surface of the dough (2), then continue to work it until it is smooth, silky, and elastic.

- Lightly dust your work surface with flour, and form the dough into a ball (see page 27). Put the dough back into your (lightly floured) bowl, cover with a cloth, and let it rest for 2 hours (3).

- Lightly dust your work surface, turn the dough out with the help of your scraper, and fold (see page 28). Form into a ball again, and then put back into your (lightly floured) bowl. Let it rest for another 12–14 hours in a cool place (10–12°C/50–53°F), such as a pantry. A cool place is better than a fridge, where the dough could get too cold to develop fully.

- Preheat the oven to 190°C/400°F.

- Remove the dough from its cool place and let it come back to room temperature for an hour or so. Lightly flour your work surface, and divide the dough into 15 x 70g (2³/₄ oz.) pieces (see page 31). Form each piece into a ball (4).

- You can either leave the balls of dough as they are (and put them straight into brioche molds), or you can place 7 balls together into your prepared pans where they will expand as they rise to form large bobbly loaves. To make the traditional brioche à tête shape that's popular in northern France, take each roll, lightly flour the side of your hand, then press into the roll about two thirds of the way across, and "saw" across it a few times to create a little "head" (5). Lift each roll up by its head, to stretch it a little, then set it down and press all around the head with your fingertips (6–7). Place in your brioche mold (8).

- If this all sounds too tricky, simply slice off the head of your ball of dough, roll it into a ball, and stick it back onto the bottom of your ball (you will need to make a little dent in the base first).

- Cover with baking cloths and let rise for 2¹/₂ hours.

- Brush with egg wash and bake the buns for 10 minutes (9). If you are baking several buns together in 1 loaf pan, you will need to turn down the heat to 180°C/250°F after 10 minutes, then bake for another 25–30 minutes until dark golden. Remove from the pan and cool on a wire rack.

FAR BRETON

This is a specialty of Brittany (Far is derived from the Latin farina, meaning flour). When I was growing up, my mother would make up a batch every couple of weeks as a snack to have after school. However, it was originally eaten by agricultural workers who took it into the fields for their lunch.

Preparation: 15 minutes **Baking:** 35–40 minutes **Freezing:** Not recommended.

Makes 1 far

You will need

400g (14oz.) prunes, pitted (about 3–3¹/₂ cups)

50g rum (¹/₂ cup)

50g (1³/₄oz.) unsalted butter, melted, for greasing (about 3¹/₂ tablespoons)

130g (4¹/₂oz.) sugar (about ²/₃ cup)

220g (8oz.) egg, (shelled weight), roughly equivalent to 4 large eggs

110g (4oz.) flour (³/₄–1 cup)

a pinch of salt

750g cold whole milk (about 3³/₄ cups)

To prepare

Soak the prunes in the rum for at least a few hours, or overnight if possible. Preheat the oven to 220°C/425°F. Grease a deep (around 4cm—2in.) 20 x 25cm (8 x 10in.) or equivalent oval earthenware dish. Brush your dish with the melted butter.

To make

● Mix the sugar and eggs together and add the flour gradually, then the salt. Whisk in the cold milk gradually to make a thin batter.

● Spoon the soaked prunes into your buttered dish, and then put it into the oven for a few minutes just to warm up the prunes. Remove from the oven and pour in the batter.

● Bake for 10 minutes, and then turn down the heat to 180°C/350°F and bake for another 25–30 minutes.

● To check that the far is ready, dip the blade of a sharp knife into cold water, and use it to pierce the middle—if the knife comes out clean, it is ready. The sides of the far will also be starting to come away from the dish. Cool completely in the dish, and then slice into pieces or use a round cutter. Serve with a cup of tea.

MR Z'S GINGERBREAD COOKIES

My Czech assistant Z introduced me to these—his real name is Zdenek, but everyone calls him Z because it's easier to pronounce. The recipe is his grandmother Maria's, and he and his family always make the cookies at Christmas time. My children like this recipe so much that we cut the dough into shapes, make little holes in each one, then thread them with ribbon after baking and hang them on the Christmas tree.

Preparation: 25 minutes **Resting:** 15–20 minutes **Baking:** 18 minutes **Freezing:** Not recommended.

Makes around 30–36

You will need

425g (15oz.) flour (about $3^1/4$ cups)

100g ($3^1/2$oz.) confectioners' sugar ($^3/4$–1 cup)

125g ($4^1/2$oz.) butter, softened ($^1/2$ cup plus 1 tbsp.)—use the wrapper for greasing the trays if necessary

100g ($3^1/2$oz.) honey (roughly $^1/3$ cup)

55g (2oz.) egg (shelled weight), roughly equivalent to 1 large egg

1 large egg yolk

1 tablespoon milk

$^1/2$ teaspoon baking soda

$^1/2$ teaspoon ground cinnamon

$^1/2$ teaspoon ground allspice

$^1/2$ teaspoon ground ginger

pinch of salt

1 egg beaten with a pinch of salt about 1 hour before it is needed, to make an egg wash

To prepare

Preheat the oven to 160°C/325°F. You will need a selection of cookie cutters and 1 or 2 baking trays, either nonstick or lined with parchment paper and lightly greased with butter.

To make

● Put all the ingredients in a mixing bowl and mix them together with your scraper to make a dough. Cover with a baking cloth and let it rest at room temperature for 15–20 minutes.

● Lightly dust your work surface with flour, and roll out the dough with a rolling pin to about 5mm ($^1/4$in.) thick. Cut it into any shapes you like (circles, stars, etc.) using a sharp knife or cutters. (If you want to hang them on the tree, make holes near the top, using a metal skewer or a very small cutter.)

● Lay the cut shapes on your prepared baking tray or trays, glaze with the egg wash, let them dry, and then glaze again. Decorate the cookies by dragging the prongs of a fork across the surface of each biscuit to form ridges.

● Bake for about 18 minutes, transfer to wire racks, and let cool completely. Thread, if you like, with ribbon.

MY BATH BUNS

When I moved to Bath, England, Jon Overton, the owner of the Sally Lunn bakery, world renowned for its Bath Buns, invited me to come and try the famous buns.

Preparation: Ferment + 30 minutes   **Resting:** 2 hours   **2nd rising:** 2–2½ hours   **Baking:** 15–18 minutes for small buns, 18–22 for large buns

Drawing on the traditions of brioche, Bath Buns are still made to the original recipe dating back over 300 years to the time when Sally Lunn, a young French refugee, arrived at the bakehouse in Bath and began baking them. I tried to bribe Jon to tell me the recipe, but of course he wasn't going to give away the secret, so I experimented and came up with my own version of the renowned sweet bun.

As this is an English recipe, albeit developed by a French girl, I like to use a good, creamy English butter. You can either make plain buns, top them with crunchy sugar crystals (apparently, the originals were topped with caraway seeds poached in sugar syrup until they crystallized), or make a fruited version—depending on whether you want to serve them on their own, or with a savory or sweet filling. You can make large ones, like the Sally Lunn buns, which are my favorite, or smaller ones.

Makes 6 large or 12 small buns

FOR THE FERMENT
You will need
125g (4½oz.) white bread flour (a scant cup)
125g water, at body temperature (about ⅔ cup)
5g fresh yeast (about 1 level tsp.)

To make
Put all the ingredients for the ferment in a mixing bowl, and mix together really well with your scraper. Cover with a baking cloth and let it rest in a warm place for 2–2½ hours.

FOR THE DOUGH
You will need
10g (⅓oz.) fresh yeast (about 2 level tsp.)
375g (13oz.) white bread flour (about 2¾ cups)
all of the ferment
125g (4½oz.) creamy English butter (½ cup + 1
    tbsp.)—use the wrapper for greasing
60g (2oz.) sugar (⅓ cup)
150g milk, at body temperature (about ¾ cup)
110g (4oz.) egg (shelled weight), roughly
    equivalent to 2 large eggs
7g (¼oz.) salt (about 1½ level tsp.)

FOR THE GLAZE
You will need
150g milk (about ¾ cup)
75g (2⅔oz.) caster sugar (about ⅓ cup)

- Again, lightly flour your work surface, turn out the dough with the help of your scraper, fold it (see page 28), and then form it back into a ball. Put back into your (lightly floured) bowl and let it rest for another hour.

- Again, lightly flour your work surface, turn out the dough and divide it into 6 large buns of 180g (6oz.), or 12 smaller ones of 90g (3oz.)—see page 31.

- Form each piece of dough into a ball (see page 27). Place on your greased baking tray or trays, allowing room to spread. Cover with a baking cloth and let rise for 2–2 1/2 hours, until double in size.

- Warm the milk for the glaze in a small pan, add the sugar, and stir well over a low heat until it dissolves. Glaze the buns well. Bake for 18–22 minutes for the large buns and 15–18 minutes for the small buns, until golden underneath and golden and plump on top.

- Take out of the oven and glaze again while still hot. Cool on wire racks.

To prepare
Preheat the oven to 180°C/375°F. Lightly grease a baking tray or trays.

To make
- Put the flour in a mixing bowl and then crumble in the yeast with your fingers. Add all the rest of the ingredients, and mix well using your scraper. When everything starts to come together into a dough, use your scraper to help you turn it out onto your work surface (don't flour it first). Work the dough (see pages 24–6) until it is smooth and silky.

- Lightly flour your work surface, and then form the dough into a ball (see page 27). Put back into your (lightly floured) mixing bowl, cover with a baking cloth and let it rest for 1 hour.

Variations

Sugar-topped buns After you have glazed your buns, press some crushed rock sugar into the top of each bun while it is still sticky.

Fruit buns Mix together 110g (about 3/4 cup) undyed glacé cherries (quartered), 110g (about 3/4 cup) candied peel, and 170g (about 1 1/4 cups) golden raisins. Follow the recipe for Bath buns, but after the dough has rested for the first time, turn it out onto your work surface (sticky-side up), and spread the fruit and peel mixture over the top. Fold the fruit into the dough and then form into a ball again and continue as before. You can top the buns with sugar crystals (see above), if you like.

ADDITIONAL RECIPES

Crème pâtissière

Makes around 700g (1¹/₂lb.). In a bowl, whisk together 6 egg yolks, 70g (¹/₃ cup) sugar and 50g (about 6 tsbp.) sifted flour. Put another 70g (¹/₃ cup) sugar into a heavy pan with 500g (about 2¹/₂ cups) whole milk and a vanilla bean (split lengthways and the seeds scraped in). Place over a low heat until the first bubble appears, and then remove from the heat. Whisk one-third of the hot milk into the egg mixture, then add the remaining two-thirds and whisk again. Pour the mixture back into your pan and put it back on the heat. Bring to a boil, stirring constantly, and then turn down the heat and simmer for a couple of minutes to cook the flour. Keep stirring all the time to ensure the cream doesn't burn on the bottom of the pan. Pour into a dish to cool. **Note:** To prevent a skin from forming, you can sprinkle a little confectioners' sugar or flakes of butter over the top.

Crème d'amande

Makes around 500g (18oz.). Beat 125g (1 cup plus 1 tbsp.) unsalted butter and 125g (²/₃ cup) sugar by hand, or mix in a food processor with a paddle, until pale and fluffy. Add 125g (1¹/₃ cups) ground almonds and mix again. Add 25g (3 tbsp.) flour and continue to mix. Finally add 2 eggs, one at a time, along with 2 large tablespoons of rum (if you like), mixing well between each addition, until the cream is light in consistency. Store in an airtight container in the fridge for up to a week.

Sugar syrup

To make
Makes around 400g (14oz.). Place 250g (about 1¹/₄ cups) water and 200g (7oz.) sugar in a heavy pan over a low heat until the sugar has dissolved. Turn up the heat and boil rapidly for 3 minutes. Take off the heat. If you like, while still warm, you can add 30g (2 tablespoons) of your favorite liqueur. Leave to cool.

Béchamel sauce

Makes around 400g (14oz.). Melt 50g (3¹/₂ tablespoons) unsalted butter over a medium heat in a heavy pan. When it has all melted and is bubbling gently, add 40g (about ¹/₃ cup) flour and whisk briskly until all of the butter has been absorbed and you have a putty-like paste that comes cleanly away from the sides of the pan. Add 300g (about 1¹/₂ cups) whole milk, a little at a time, whisking continuously to ensure that no lumps form. Once all the milk has been added and you have a smooth sauce, cook over a low to medium heat until it starts to bubble. Cook for another minute. Season to taste with sea salt (or kosher salt), freshly ground black pepper, and a little ground nutmeg. Let it cool. **Note:** For a richer sauce, add 50–80g (¹/₂–³/₄ cup) grated cheese (Cheddar or Gruyère work well) to the sauce while it is over the heat, making sure it melts completely.

5

FACT & FICTION

So much is written about bread—is it good for you? Is it fattening? Does it contain too much salt? Why are so many people complaining about allergies to wheat and gluten? Personally I think that homemade bread is one of the best foods you and your family can eat, and in this chapter I'll tell you why... as well as giving you a few quick and easy recipes for leftover bread, so you can make the most of every crumb of goodness.

ABOUT BREAD

Good bread is good for you; bad bread is less good for you—it's as simple as that. The same applies with any food—a burger made freshly with excellent beef is a great thing; a cheap, processed burger full of additives and fillers isn't.

Some of the "products" you find in the bakery section of supermarkets and shops don't even deserve to be called bread in my eyes. They should have a name of their own. What makes me especially angry is the idea of marketing crustless bread to children and their parents. As an experiment I took a slice of one of the new "breads" priding itself on being "crustless," scrunched it in my hands and passed it around one of my classes, asking them to identify it. "Dough" said everyone. That's how under-baked such "bread" has to be, to be crustless.

There is a story I tell when people come to my bread classes for the first time— my shrimp sandwich story. Imagine, I say, you pack a sandwich on Sunday night, ready to take to work on Monday morning. You take 2 slices of soft, white, pre-sliced sandwich bread, you smear on some spread from a tub, perhaps full of hydrogenated fat, add some low-fat mayonnaise (trying to be healthy), then you put in some cucumber, full of water, shrimp (that were probably frozen) fresh from their plastic container, and some iceberg lettuce. You wrap the sandwich in a

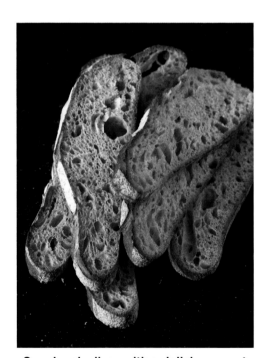

Sourdough slices with a delicious crust

plastic bag, and leave it in the fridge overnight. The next morning you put it, inside its plastic bag, inside a plastic box and go to the office. You leave your box to ferment on the side of your desk for a few hours. By 1pm you start to feel hungry. You remove your plastic bag from your plastic box, make sure you have a bottle of spring water to drink— after all, you are trying to be healthy. You take a bite of your now soggy sandwich and, after the first chew, you feel the stodge sticking to the top of your palate. So you have a glug of water to unstick it, and it plummets to the bottom of your stomach. And so you go on until you have finished your delicious sandwich. Half an hour later you start to feel heavy, a bit sleepy, not very comfortable in your stomach: "Bread is bad for me," you say... "I must give it up."

By now people are laughing or wincing because they recognize, if not all, at least some of the story. Bread gets such a bad name and yet it is not only the kind of bread we buy, but the things we do to it, that make us feel as though we have a stone sitting in our stomachs.

What goes into bread?

The way we feel about bread, its place in our lives, and what goes into making it, depends very much on which country we are in, and its cultural background. Imagine these scenarios. Jean-Pierre and Jean-François are sitting on a wall in a square in a town somewhere in France, each with a crusty baguette under his arm, having stopped off for a chat on their way back from the bakery. You can just imagine them breaking off a piece of baguette to nibble on as they talk—it's just too tempting not to. Now imagine Tom and Harry sitting on a wall in a square in a town somewhere in England, each with a soft, sliced white loaf inside a sealed plastic bag. Somehow the idea of nibbling on that doesn't seem so attractive.

In a similar vein, if you were to ask someone in France to name 10 chefs and 10 bakers, the chances are they would know the names of every baker in their locality. What they would be much hazier about would be the names of the chefs, since the idea of the chef as a star has never really taken hold there in the same way as in England where anyone could reel off a host of famous chefs' names, but they would struggle to name anyone who bakes bread locally. It all comes down to how much you value bread in your life.

When I ask people in England whether they ever read the label on a loaf or on the bakery shelf in a supermarket, they are surprised that I even ask. Bread is bread, they say. While other foods may be full of additives that they would prefer to avoid, bread is something people feel they can trust. Yet if you read the label on most commercial bread, made using a quick process in comparison to traditional methods, you will be amazed at the litany of emulsifiers, flour treatment agents, preservatives, fats, and so on.

Some people say they buy whole-wheat bread because "mass-produced white bread isn't that nutritious." But whole-wheat bread produced by the big bakeries is made in exactly the same fast-track way and can actually be worse for you, because whole-wheat bread—unless it's made slowly and carefully—can be quite heavy and even more indigestible. I wish big bakeries would slow the process down, bake for longer, and invest in skills. But for this to happen we all need to be prepared to pay a little more for our bread.

Mass-produced 'crustless' loaf

Crust and saliva

Poor-quality bread, eaten in vast quantities and barely chewed, can cause digestive problems, but good wholesome bread, made with natural ingredients and, above all, a good crust, can actually help the digestion.

Digestion begins almost as soon as we begin to see and smell good food. Even before we eat it, the body is producing enzymes and other secretions necessary for digestion. But once we start to eat, it is chewing that is the real key. When we chew properly, the salivary glands secrete enzymes that start breaking down the carbohydrates or sugars, ready for absorption into the bloodstream further down the digestive tract.

The problem with many of our over-processed foods today, including bread, is that very little chewing is required. We are all geared up to fast food and fast mealtimes, so instead of relaxing over our food and eating slowly, we grab a bite on the go—stressed, rushing, swallowing as quickly as we can, barely chewing. For our stomachs, it must feel like 500 emails arriving in our in-boxes at the same time. They say Prime Minister Gladstone chewed every mouthful of his food 30 times, which probably drove anyone eating with him crazy, but he lived until he was 90 years old.

The salt issue

As I mentioned in Chapter 1, there is so much worry these days over eating too much salt that it is easy to forget that we can't survive without it in our diet. Salt is critical for regulating the hydration of the body. It controls how much water passes in and out of our bodies' cells, cleansing them and extracting toxins and waste. Provided we are physically active and eat a balanced diet with plenty of fresh fruit and vegetables, salt levels shouldn't normally be a worry; it is when we take no exercise and eat a diet laden with salt "hidden" in processed foods that every extra gram becomes crucial.

Remember, though, that what we are talking about here is unrefined, natural sea salt or rock salt (such as kosher salt), which is very different from table salt (sodium chloride). This is produced by heating the salt, a process which strips the raw product of all but a handful of the 80 or so minerals and other chemicals found in its natural state. So when you bake, always use natural sea or rock salt (or kosher salt). In my kitchen I like to experiment with a variety such as sel gris (wet, gray colored sea salt—top left opposite), fine sea salt (top right), fleur de sel (bottom right) and smoked Welsh sea salt flakes (bottom left).

It is hard to achieve good bread with a depth of flavor and a serious crust without salt. And remember that although it might seem that you are adding a lot of salt to your mixing bowl, in proportion to the other ingredients, the amount of salt is relatively small. I had a laboratory analysis done of 100g of my sourdough— that's two substantial slices—which shows that it contains 1.2g of salt. By comparison 100g of cornflakes can contain 2g salt. And I know which I would prefer for breakfast. Also, you have to look at the whole picture. A typical processed white loaf can contain around 3.8g of sugar per 100g and 2.5g of fat per 100g, whereas my sourdough clocks up 2g sugar per 100g and 1.1g of fat (which are naturally occuring) and not an additive in sight.

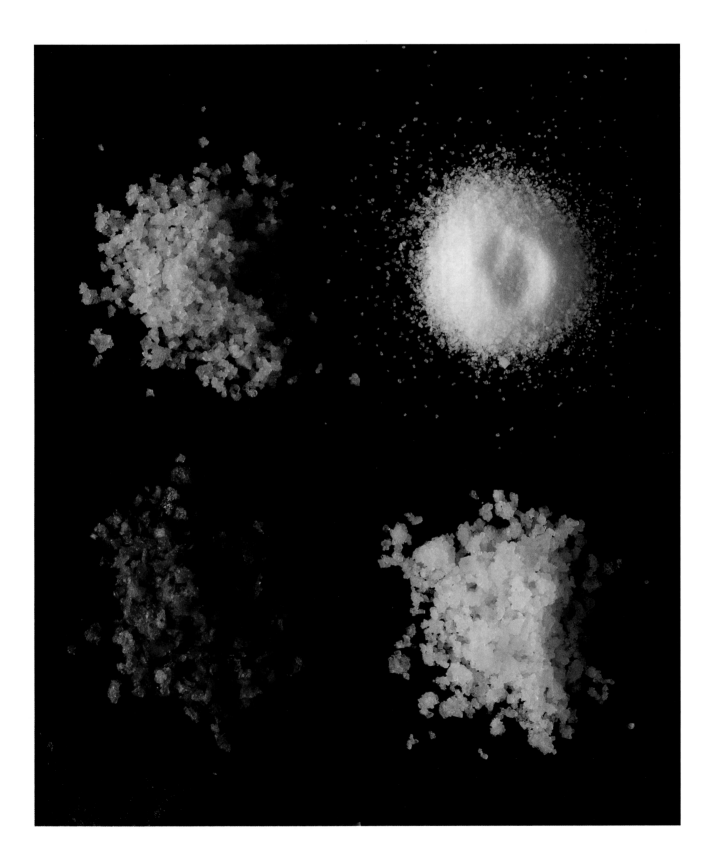

Why hot bread isn't good for you

Always let your bread cool down properly after you take it out of the oven before you eat it, or it can be indigestible. When it first comes out of the oven, bread is full of moisture from the steam generated during baking. The more dense the loaf, the longer it will take to cool down, so if you want bread to eat quickly, choose one with a high ratio of crust to crumb. In scientific terms, the starch molecules in hot bread are tightly grouped together and difficult for the enzymes in our saliva to break down. This means that they go into the stomach still clumped together, putting the digestive system under pressure and often causing discomfort, which many people mistake for wheat allergy.

The truth about wheat issues

Many people talk about having a wheat allergy, when what they are actually experiencing is some kind of wheat sensitivity—similar to the "shrimp sandwich effect" I talked about on page 146. True wheat allergy is a serious and violent reaction to wheat, but it is actually very rare and only affects about 0.5% of the population. What is more common is coeliac disease, an inflammatory condition of the gastrointestinal tract, caused by gluten (a protein found in wheat). Coeliac disease is a permanent condition which, according to the charity Coeliac UK, affects around 1 in 100 people, who have to follow a gluten-free diet.

Wheat *sensitivity*—as opposed to wheat *allergy*—affects around 15% of the population (about 1 in 7, though that makes it far less common than reactions to dairy food, which are estimated to affect as many as 3 in 4 people). Too much of any food, bread included, can cause this kind of sensitivity, and by reducing the amount you eat, or cutting it out of your diet altogether for a while, you can often put things right and start eating it again. Often, though, I would say that if people who are eating a lot of processed bread try eating good homemade bread or bread from a self-respecting baker who uses the old-fashioned, slow process and no "improvers" and additives, they will notice the difference.

Which bread?

In France, we have a bread for every occasion—a small ficelle for breakfast, a baguette at lunchtime, le pain for the family in the evening. We don't expect such breads to last for more than a day. A pain de levain or pain de campagne, on the other hand, is bought to last for 2–3 days, to slice at first, and then to cut up into croûtons, to toast, to make tartines, or to put in slices into soup, or a pot-au-feu. No bread in France is ever wasted.

Toast is simply another, specific way to eat bread. The point about it is that the bread should be left to dry out for a few days to give the toast a good, crunchy texture and this makes it more digestible. If you toast very fresh or doughy commercial bread, which still has a lot of moisture in it, the toasting has the same effect on your stomach as eating hot bread straight from the oven.

Of course you can enjoy the breads in this book in any way you like, though I have my favorite matches. I am now "so English" that I especially love Sourdough with the perfect Ploughman's: real Cheddar, homemade pickles and chutney, crisp salad leaves, and chunks of sweet/sharp English apples (pictured opposite).

IDEAS FOR LEFTOVER BREAD

Never throw away bread that is a few days old, just because it has lost a little of its moisture. It is invaluable to use in all sorts of ways.

Tartine

A tartine is a slice of bread. However, these days it is more usually used to describe the French equivalent of the Italian bruschetta, and uses a toasted slice of lovely sourdough, pain de campagne, or another good rustic bread, topped with whatever you like—in this case, creamy mushrooms.

Serves 4

You will need

2 tablespoons olive oil

1 large shallot or 2 small ones, finely chopped

1 clove garlic, crushed

500g (18oz.) field or wild mushrooms, sliced

1/3 cup brandy (or red wine)

4 heaped tablespoons crème fraîche

small bunch of parsley, finely chopped

4 slices sourdough (see page 54), or other good
    rustic bread, a few days old,

To make

● Heat the oil in a frying pan, add the shallots and garlic and sauté over a high heat until lightly browned. Add the mushrooms and stir well. Add the brandy or wine and let it ignite—be very careful when you do this. Cook for 30 seconds, and then remove the pan from the heat and stir in the crème fraîche.

● Put the pan back over a low heat and cook gently for 5 minutes.

● Meanwhile, lightly toast your slices of bread.

● Add the chopped parsley to the pan, and stir it through. To serve, spoon the mushroom mixture over the slices of toasted bread.

Croûtons

To make croûtons, cut your stale bread into equal-sized cubes. Fry them very gently in a little butter and olive oil over a low heat. Drain well on paper towels and use the croûtons to scatter onto salads or soups.

Breadcrumbs

In France it is second nature to put your leftover bread into a food processor, and then sift it so that you have some fine crumbs and some that are a bit more coarse. You can keep them in a food bag in the freezer and use them from frozen for coating fish or cutlets, for binding fish cakes or forcemeats and stuffings, or even for coating a goat cheese before baking it (in which case, I would usually use finer breadcrumbs).

French toast

Take 4 slices of stale bread or brioche. Beat 2 eggs with 2 tablespoons sugar, 4 tablespoons milk, and a good pinch of ground cinnamon. Melt some butter in a large frying pan. When it is foaming, dip your bread into the eggy mixture and fry on both sides until golden brown. Take out and drain on paper towels, and dust with superfine or granulated sugar.

Garlic bread

You will need

4 cloves garlic
a small bunch of curly parsley (I prefer the taste of
    curly parsley over flat parsley for garlic bread)
250g (9oz.) butter, softened (1 cup plus 2 tbsp.)
a squeeze of fresh lemon juice
4 thick slices of good crusty bread preferably (or
    any leftover bread)

To make

● Preheat the oven to 210–220°C/400–425°F. Peel the garlic, cut in two lengthways, and remove any of the green germ (which is the part that some people find indigestible). Crush the cloves of garlic with the back of a knife, and chop very finely until you have a paste or use a garlic crusher. Finely chop the parsley.

● Put the butter into a food processor and blitz. Add the garlic and blitz again. Add the parsley and a few drops of lemon juice and blitz one more time. Spread onto your bread, and then put into the oven until the butter has melted and the bread is golden (about 5–8 minutes).

Le pudding

We used to make this in the bakery when I was an apprentice, using all the leftover bits of bread, cake, croissant, pain aux raisins, and pain au chocolat. I suppose it's the French version of bread and butter pudding, but more dense and very addictive. You need a good mixture of bread and patisserie.

Makes enough for 6 generous portions

You will need

about 500g (18oz.) leftover bread, croissants, etc.
300g (11oz.) crème pâtissière (see page 143)—
    about 1¹/4–1¹/2 cups
200g (7oz.) golden raisins (about 1¹/4–1¹/2 cups)
4–5 tablespoons rum
butter, for greasing
a little confectioners' sugar, for dusting

To make

Preheat the oven to 180°C/375°F. Put all the stale bread, etc. into a food processor with a paddle and switch it on to a slow speed until well crumbed but still quite rough. Transfer to a bowl and add the crème pâtissière, raisins, and rum, and mix to a creamy stodge. Line a deep tray with lightly buttered baking paper and pile in the mixture, but don't smooth it too much on top, since you want it to be nice and crisp, with uneven peaks. Bake for 35–45 minutes until crisp and golden on top. Let it cool before dusting with confectioners' sugar and cutting into chunks.

SUPPLIERS & SOURCES

Equipment

All of the specialist baking equipment including proving baskets, couches, linen baking cloths, lames, scrapers and baking peels can be obtained by mail order or in person from The Bertinet Kitchen. Other items can be found in good general kitchenware shops.

The Bertinet Kitchen
12 St Andrew's Terrace
Bath
England
BA1 2QR
01225 445531
info@thebertinetkitchen.com
www.thebertinetkitchen.com

Ingredients

FLOURS

U.K.

Shipton Mill
Long Newnton
Tetbury
Gloucestershire
GL8 8RP
01666 505050
enquiries@shipton-mill.com
www.shipton-mill.com

Sharpham Park (spelt)
01458 844080
info@sharphampark.com
www.sharphampark.com

Bacheldre Watermill
Churchstoke
Montgomery
Powys
SY15 6TE
01588 620489
info@bacheldremill.co.uk
www.bacheldremill.co.uk

U.S.

Anson Mills
www.ansonmills.com

Aarowhead Mills
www.arrowheadmills.com

Bobs Red Mill Natural Foods
www.bobsredmill.com

Dakota Prairie Organic Flour Co.
www.dakota-prairie.com

Fairhaven Organic Flour Mill
www.fairhavenflour.com

King Arthur Flour
www.kingarthurflour.com

Rock Creek Organics
www.rockcreekorganics.com

For more information on red Cabernet flour, see www.viniferaforlife.com

FRESH YEAST

Yeast can be purchased from most instore bakeries on request. You may also be able to get it from a health food store or your local delicatessen may be able to order it for you.

PREMIUM SAKE

Isake sake is available at www.isake.co.uk and

CONVERSION TABLE

VOLUME

5ml	1 tsp.
10ml	1 dessert spoon
15ml	1 tbsp.
30ml	1fl. oz. or 2 tbsp.
60ml	2fl. oz.
75ml	2½fl. oz.
90ml	3fl. oz.
120ml	4fl. oz. (½ cup)
150ml	5fl. oz.
180ml	6fl. oz.
210ml	7fl. oz.
240ml	8fl. oz. (1 cup)
250ml	8½fl. oz.
300ml	10fl. oz.
360ml	12fl. oz.
410ml	14fl. oz.
440ml	15fl. oz.
470ml	16fl. oz. (2 cups)
500ml)	17fl. oz.
600ml	20fl. oz.
700ml	3 cups
850ml	3½ cups
1 liter	4 cups
1.2 liters	5 cups
1.5 liters	6⅓ cups
2 liters	8½ cups

WEIGHT

10g	⅓oz.
20g	¾oz.
30g	1oz.
60g	2oz.
70g	2½oz.
85g	3oz.
100g	3½oz.
110g	4oz. (¼lb.)
150g	5oz.
175g	6oz.
200g	7oz.
225g	8oz. (½lb.)
250g (¼kg)	9oz.
285g	10oz.
340g	12oz. (¾lb.)
400g	14oz.
450g	1lb.
500g (½kg)	18oz.
570g	1¼lb.
680g	1½lb.
900g	2lb.
1kg	2¼lb.
1.1kg	2½lb.
1.3kg	3lb.
1.5kg	3lb. 5oz.
1.6kg	3½lb.
1.8kg	4lb.
2kg	4½lb.
2.2kg	5lb.

MEASUREMENTS

3mm	⅛in.
5mm	¼in.
1cm	½in.
2cm	¾in.
2.5cm	1in.
3cm	1¼in.
4cm	1½in.
5cm	2in.
6cm	2½in.
7.5cm	2¾in.
9cm	3½in.
10cm	4in.
11.5cm	4½in.
12.5cm	5in.
15cm	6in.
17cm	6½in.
18cm	7in.
20.5cm	8in.
23cm	9in.
25cm	10in.
30.5cm	11in.

INDEX

An Hachette UK Company
www.hachette.co.uk

First published in Great Britain in 2007 by Kyle Books, an imprint of Kyle Cathie Ltd
Carmelite House, 50 Victoria Embankment, London EC4Y 0DZ
www.octopusbooksusa.com

This edition published in 2020

ISBN: 978 0 85783 916 9

Distributed in the US by Hachette Book Group, 1290 Avenue of the Americas, 4th and 5th Floors, New York, NY 10104

Distributed in Canada by Canadian Manda Group, 664 Annette St., Toronto, Ontario, Canada M6S 2C8

Copy editor: Catherine Ward
Proofreader: Stephanie Evans
Design: Jenny Semple
Photography: Jean Cazals
Props: Sue Rowlands
Production: Sha Huxtable and Alice Holloway

* except photographs on pages 7 and 8: The Bertinet Kitchen

Printed and bound in China

10 9 8 7 6 5 4 3 2 1